BLOOMSBURYGO

100 MUST-READ

BOOKSFORMEN

Stephen E Andrews and Duncan Bowis

Foreword by Toby Litt

A & C Black • London

First published 2008
A & C Black Publishers Limited
38 Soho Square
London W1D 3HB
www.acblack.com

ISBN: 978 0 7136 8873 3

A CIP catalogue record for this book is available from the British Library.

This book is produced using paper that is made from wood grown in managed, sustainable forests. It is natural, renewable and recyclable. The logging and manufacturing processes conform to the environmental regulations of the country of origin.

Typeset in 8.5pt on 12pt Meta-Light

Printed and bound in the UK by
CPI Bookmarque, Croydon, CR0 4TD

CONTENTS

FOREWORD

As readers, men get a pretty bad press. (Men get a pretty bad press generally, but that's another issue.)

I'm a writer, and I feel that by being a writer I'm following my vocation. As a reader, though, I feel a lot less definite, a lot more vulnerable. I know this is massively paradoxical. If I hadn't become a reader, there is far less chance that I'd have discovered novels, started writing, become a writer, etc. However, it's hard for me to look back and see myself turning out any differently. At the same time, I know that there are books I needed to encounter to be convinced, or (more importantly) re-convinced, that reading was something I wanted to spend my time doing. After all, there were my friends, my skateboard, my computer games...

For a while, I've been intending to construct an Autobibliography (to be accompanied by an Autodiscography). Here's a kind of rough draft. Please note: these aren't things that were read to me; these are things I picked up myself.

In the beginning was the television. My parents used to warn me that I'd turn into Mike Teavee from ***Charlie and the Chocolate Factory***. They swore that if I sat *that* close to the screen, I'd first get square eyes and then go blind. (Perhaps because they saw TV as a form of masturbation.) They even threatened to throw 'the gogglebox' out. I was as distressed by the image of this – a smashed TV lying alongside our dustbins – as by anything I could imagine, including the total extinction of pandas.

I was also reading, though. But what I started with wasn't books. It was ***The Beano, The Dandy*** and ***Whizzer and Chips***. Then I discovered Marvel comics – ***The Fantastic Four, The Silver Surfer***. (I especially loved the ads at the back, for Hostess Twinkies – which I still haven't tasted. American kids seemed to live extremely desirable lives.) I was also keen on British comics like ***Commando*** and ***Battle***. When ***2000AD*** came out, I bought it from issue one. It was on order for me at the local post office – my name biro'd on the top corner.

Then I started to pick books out of boxes at jumble sales. I read ***Splinter of the Mind's Eye*** – the first ever Star Wars spin-off book. I read ***The Pan Books of Horror Stories***. And then, around eleven years old, I journeyed through ***The Lord of the Rings***. Finishing this was the Rubicon. If I could get to the end of something *that* big, I could read anything in the world. I had books beaten.

Looking back, it seems almost a logical chain of escalation – from captions to stories to novels to multivolume epics. (***Dune*** followed soon after, though I was defeated by ***Dune Messiah***.) But I realise how fragile each of these links were. And, even now, I'm hit by periods when I read listlessly, unaffected by the words on the page. So the question isn't just *What should I read next?* but *What should I read that will make me love reading again?*

It's not possible that I'll ever feel the same sense of triumph I did when setting aside J.R.R. Tolkien's third hefty volume. But I know there are books out there which make we want to turn to myself and say, *Isn't this just the best thing ever? These words on the page that belong equally to writer, reader and whoever else happens upon them*. I know there are lots of these great books – it's just a question of finding them.

This book is intended to help me, and – more importantly – you, do just that.

And if this book is going to do that, then you'll have to start to trust it.

Perhaps you'll begin by looking up a couple of books you know, to see if you agree with what the authors say about them.

Or perhaps you'll read an entry and then go out and buy a novel you wouldn't otherwise have read, and you'll discover an entirely new author, a new way of looking at things, and you'll willingly dip back in for another go.

Already, probably, you'll have flicked through to have a quick look at which hundred books they've chosen. Maybe there are things you wanted to make sure were included. Hunter S. Thompson? Check. Couldn't do this without Hunter. Or maybe you were looking for surprises. Spike Milligan? Well, I suppose so. Maybe you've already started up a pub-corner argument. ***Islands in the Stream*** instead of ***The Sun Also Rises***? Come on, guys. Deke Leonard but no Elmore Leonard? Hell no! Or maybe you've been nodding in list-boy approval. Klaus Kinski and Che Guevara. Oh, yes! M. John Harrison *and* Georges Bataille. Bingo!

But it seems to me, after hanging around it for a while, that this is a book you *can* trust. Mainly because its authors have a clear idea of what men are and what they generally like to read.

In the end, you may feel that you're a little off-centre from their chosen heartland – in whichever direction. I'd be really surprised, though, if you a. have gonads and b. fell outside their boundaries completely.

Toby Litt

ABOUT THIS BOOK

Our purpose in writing this book was not to try to establish a definitive list of the hundred 'best' books that would appeal to all men. Given the diversity of literary tastes amongst men from all walks of life, such an aim would not only be hubristic, but insulting. To be a man is first and foremost to be an individual, as until recently, the upper hand men have undoubtedly enjoyed from time immemorial has allowed us to define ourselves not primarily by our gender, but by the freedom of choice to select our own identities that came as our male birthright. One consequence of this freedom of choice is the common observation that one man's unassailable canon is another man's garbage. Popularity polls and bestseller charts are equally suspect: how many of us have discovered a book that we strongly believe would appeal to others, to find that it has languished in undeserved obscurity? All too often important tomes go unnoticed amongst massively over-hyped works by the current critic's darlings. We think that most thinking men are healthily cynical and unlikely to be swayed by mere popularity, preferring the taint of maverick individuality instead.

Therefore, we have sought to recommend one hundred excellent books that we believe the majority of contemporary men will probably enjoy and relate to. In making our selection, we relied on our extensive expertise as readers and bibliophiles and the diversity of our experiences as men. Also, over the decades we both spent as booksellers, we encountered thousands of readers and discussed with them numerous books in all genres, so we feel confident in stating that although not every volume described here will appeal to every man, we think that most readers will find echoes of their own personal experiences of masculinity reflected in the voices of the majority of authors we've chosen to represent.

The individual book entries are arranged alphabetically by author. Non-fiction titles are indicated thus: **(NF)**. In selecting non-fiction, we have primarily stuck to personal narrative forms such as autobiography and biography, although you will find other categories of non-fiction represented in our choices and in the 'Read on a theme' boxes that are scattered throughout the text after appropriately related entries: these lists are designed to help you explore particular masculine literary themes in greater depth. In the fiction entries we delineate the plot of each novel, while aiming to avoid too many 'spoilers'. We offer some value judgements as well as information about the author's career and their place in the history of literature (or their chosen field if they are primarily known for achievement outside writing). We have also included the original publication date of each title. Significant film and television adaptations (with dates of release) are noted where applicable.

Each entry is followed by a 'Read on' list that includes books by the same author (including any sequels and prequels), books by stylistically similar writers or books on a theme relevant to the entry. In a small number of cases we have included full series listings arranged in order of internal chronology (i.e. in the order of events in the fictional world the author has set his stories in), as we're all too familiar with the difficulty of finding accurate bibliographies for lengthy sagas. Finally, the symbol ›› before a writer's name (e.g. ›› Charles Bukowski) indicates that one or more of their books is covered in the A to Z author entries.

When considering titles for inclusion, we took the following factors into account: deserved popularity, cult status, critical acclaim, originality, unfair obscurity, historical significance and even personal preference. Even more important than all these were the responses of male readers themselves, for example, we have often found that some books favoured by critics and experts are not as well received by readers as titles the academics and collectors tend to underplay. Sometimes we found the converse to be true.

Except in a very small number of cases, we have generally eschewed Classics (by this we primarily mean widely acclaimed masterpieces published before 1900 now issued in imprints such as Penguin Classics and Oxford World's Classics). By definition such works have universal appeal that reaches beyond gender boundaries. Additionally, almost all the Classics we considered for inclusion in this volume were already covered expertly by Nick Rennison in ***100 Must-Read Classic Novels*** and ***100 Must-Read Life-Changing Novels*** (such as *Don Quixote, Crime & Punishment, The Brothers Karamazov, Moby Dick, Germinal, The Count of Monte Cristo* and modern classics such as *The Outsider, A Farewell To Arms, The Great Gatsby* and *Hunger* plus the works of Conrad, Steinbeck and Kerouac). We have also avoided science fiction (except in two instances), again because it is extensively covered in ***100 Must-Read Science Fiction Novels***. Instead, we have included some excellent general fiction titles by writers best known for their SF and fantasy. We have also included some works by authors primarily associated with crime fiction, as we felt some important titles of particular interest to men were not included in ***100 Must-Read Crime Novels***, especially in the areas of noir fiction – that step outside traditional detection tales. Graphic novels are represented with two titles.

We have generally avoided formulaic thrillers and chunky A-format paperback 'bestsellers' as such books already command plenty of attention, aimed as they are at the mass market – you only have to look at the chart section of your local bookshop to find these. We believe that our readers can quite happily make their own decisions when shopping for techno-thrillers and 'beach reads' by popular authors like Stephen King, Wilbur Smith, Dan Brown and John Grisham, plus we wanted to point you towards authors you may not have heard of that you'll enjoy even more.

In all cases bar one (the inestimable Jack London – a man's man if ever there was one), we have chosen to represent authors by a single book. Because men's writing is not a genre, we have felt liberated from the requirement to conform to any existing canon and have instead focused on selecting titles that we feel illustrate the male experience in all its facets. Consequently, we have covered themes as diverse as sex, war, work, gambling, drinking, sport, fatherhood, responsibility, irresponsibility, adventure and many other aspects of masculinity. We have even included a small number of works by women and wished we could have included more, but, after all, this *is* a book for boys by boys. Incidentally, according to a survey in the London ***Times*** (June 2004) carried out on behalf of a major publisher, eighty five per cent of women said they would be attracted to a man who talked about literature. They also stated that they would judge a man by what kind of books he preferred. What more incentive do you need to get reading?

Regarding availability, the vast majority of the titles we've included are in print either in the UK or USA at the time of going to press, but please be aware that books can become unavailable at any time. Just ask your local bookshop to help you find anything that seems to be elusive, or visit second-hand or online booksellers such as Abebooks to find used or collectable copies of titles that are currently out of print.

If we've excluded your favourite male writer, we're probably being robustly iconoclastic by slotting in another author we feel you will enjoy as well, so please forgive us – our intention is to help you discover more great page-turners you might have missed, not to disrespect your idols. We'll state again that many other brilliant writers are covered in other volumes in this series. Although we'd be hard pressed to come up with a convincing definition of contemporary man, we are nevertheless confident that our selection of books will strike a chord with anyone bold enough to label himself as such. These are the kind of works that any of your mates might recommend while you share a round at the pub, while you wait for kick-off on the terraces or as you sit drinking espresso in a music store café, tearing the shrink-wrap from that pile of remastered CDs you've just purchased.

ACKNOWLEDGEMENTS

The authors would like to thank the following individuals for their support, inspiration and suggestions:

Georgina Bowis, Patricia Jones, Beebie, Nick Assirati, Patrick Bishop, Andrew 'Bomber' Borgelin, Vincent Cassar, Mark Denton, Martyn Folkes, Indi Garcher, Ben Hamper, Laura Hassan at Jonathan Cape, Michael Heatley at Northside Press, Neil Laing, Kate Leeming, Colin Litster, Toby Litt, Clare Mitchell, Nick Newport, Suzi Williamson, Rachel and Philip Owen, Nick Rennison, Jenny Ridout, Judy Tither, Peter Waterman, Rebecca and Mark Williams, and everyone else at A & C Black.

INTRODUCTION

What does being a man mean today? Some decades after revolutionary feminism swept the Western world, many of us are confused by our role as males in the postmodern scheme of things. In a world where it is deeply patronising to open a door for a lady and unforgivably unreconstructed to turn your head to look at her retreating backside, we men easily become perplexed. We're encouraged to tolerate advertisements for moisturiser aimed at us instead of our wives and expected to be comfortable spending quality time with our offspring in the baby changing room of Marks & Spencer when we'd rather be sinking a pint. We sometimes find ourselves irritatingly redefined by the press as 'New Men' or 'Metrosexuals'. We are often told we possess little understanding of feelings, that we fail to notice many of the finer emotional nuances of interpersonal behaviour that are immediately recognised by women. Most of our partners are tolerant of our inability to grasp the impact of tiny gestures, the miniscule variations in voice-tone inflection and the subtle semiotics of small alterations in facial expressions. After all, they know we haven't got a clue, as we're only blokes. No longer the established masters in a society that is not even vaguely patriarchal any more, our status is more uncertain than it has ever been. Young men have an even tougher time as they notice the confused state their fathers and peers are in. Is it insensitive of them to read ***Loaded*** and sad to watch ***Top Gear***?

But why should we men feel perpetually guilty? Accusations of our emotional short-sightedness may be true sometimes. But they are also arguably incorrect when considered objectively. To say that men have no feelings is itself unperceptive: better to recognise the reality that men often experience quite different feelings to those women are subject to. If we are to have sexual equality, then there must be respect for our diversity as genders (not to mention our diversity as individuals). The very word 'diversity' extends from the word difference, so to achieve egalitarianism, we must acknowledge our contrasting gender identities. We don't celebrate diversity by forcing everyone to be the same; instead we maintain diversity by having the courage to tolerate acceptable differences by allowing them to flourish, which is why we have written a book that is aimed exclusively at men. Within these pages, gentlemen, you don't have to feel guilty.

There may be exceptions to every rule, but – in case you haven't noticed – men and women *are* fundamentally different from each other. This may be a generalisation, but it is nonetheless an inescapable fact. Arguments about superiority or inferiority are fruitless, as our varying skills and abilities as genders show us to be complimentary beings – hopefully both men and women can concur that in some arenas, we are unequally matched and that as adults we should learn to live with this happily. Our contrasting natures more often than not please both sexes, as many men (though not all) celebrate these gender battles by falling in love, forming partnerships and having children. But it has become fashionable over the past thirty years to deny psychological gender differences and to claim they are socially constructed 'learned behaviours' instead of the product of biological processes. It's important to note that the nature versus nurture debate is a misleading over-simplification, as anyone can confirm from observation and research that a combination of biological and environmental factors can both be important in influencing the characters of individuals to varying degrees. For example, while some scientific research suggests that some men have a predisposition towards homosexuality due to the particular concentration of certain hormones that washed over their foetus in the womb at crucial stages of development (the biological factor that determines much of our gender identity, all foetuses being morphologically female until this stage) other men claim they turned out gay because of the way they were brought up.

Perhaps both chromosomes and conditions play inseparable parts in making us who we are as individuals, but there is little doubt that the political correctness of recent years has influenced a bias against the scientific facts regarding the significance of biological factors in dictating some of our behaviour. To learn more about the disparity in brain chemistry between men and women, about how intrauterine hormonal events shape how male or female our brains and bodies become and why men and women generally behave differently in many respects, read ***Why Men Don't Iron*** by Anne and Bill Moir (1998) and ***The Female Brain*** by Louann Brizendine (2006). Otherwise, take it from us that neurochemistry offers the most convincing arguments for the inescapable differences between men and women, most of them centring around the fact that men generally have ten times as much testosterone racing around their bodies as do women. So we men shouldn't feel bad because we prefer getting stuck into a scrum down or crate-digging at a record fair instead of debating what colour curtains we should purchase for the guest bedroom. Although women are affected by testosterone too, their body chemistry is demonstrably more strongly affected by other hormones, resulting in a definite tendency toward nest-building and nurturing instead of the more pronounced single-mindedness and competitive behaviour common in men.

But what has this all this gender-fixated stuff got to do with books?

Just as men and women often experience and respond to life in differing ways, they may also react to words differently. Deborah Cameron's ***The Myth of Mars and Venus*** (2007) disagrees with this claim, aiming to undermine the beliefs of evolutionary psychologists regarding the supposed differences between men and women's use of words. Cameron's avoidance of neurochemistry (you won't find the word 'testosterone' in the index of her book) and focus on linguistic research is firmly in the nurture camp beloved of modern feminism and sociology. We, however, follow the argument that nature remains just as important as upbringing. After all, although there are many writers enjoyed by both men and women, anyone who has worked around books will recognise that there are writers who are generally considered to be authors of 'women's reads' or 'books for blokes'. Novels in niches such as 'Chick Lit', are pretty clearly aimed at the female market, while A-format ghost-written paperbacks by former SAS operatives with guns on the jackets are doubtless intended for a testosterone-fuelled demographic. Perhaps more crucially, it's interesting to note that when a recent poll of the books men felt most affecting was run (by a team of female researchers), that the clear winner was Albert Camus' arid existentialist masterpiece ***The Outsider*** (1942), the iconic tale of an indifferent man drawn to murder. So while the ladies voted overwhelmingly for the majestic, slow-burning passion and quiet commitment of classic romance ***Jane Eyre*** (1847) as their favourite read, men opted en masse for contingency, solipsism and ambivalence.

According to some neuroscientists, men's verbal ability is less developed than that of women, whose allegedly superior linguistic abilities leave most boys behind during childhood reading progress tests. Despite this, we men can appear to be complex creatures when it comes to engaging us with prose: for example, ***The Outsider*** may be direct in its storytelling approach, but it engages with extremely important philosophical issues relevant to how one should live life without flinching away from the bleak and the downright difficult. Camus' masterpiece confronts these issues head-on through the outlook of his protagonist, Meursault: his mother doesn't die and the Arab isn't killed just for our entertainment, but to make us question higher morality and how we deal with our reality in practical terms. The popularity of ***The Outsider*** amongst male readers not only suggests how serious our inner concerns are, but how readily men relate to Meursault's indifference – like most of us, he finds it easy to retreat into his cave and be solitary, whether to contemplate the meaning of life or to enjoy it for its own sake. Comparatively, it might be argued that *Jane Eyre* might indicate that many female readers have less complex philosophical aspirations – for all her intelligence and sensitivity, Jane could be regarded as little more than a woman who wants to marry a strong, complex bloke. To be fair, this view disregards the social role man imposed upon women in the Brontës' days (and the oppression females endured for much of human history), but Eyre's character and aspirations still speak to many contemporary females, so perhaps this is what some women want out of a book – romance with a small R, something we men often look down upon. Or is it just that Brontë appeals because women apparently have better hearing than men and are often cited by behaviourists as superior listeners and conversationalists, meaning that they appreciate fine character studies more than male readers, being more aware of the complexities of relationships than we guys, consequently making them both better writers and more sophisticated readers? Perhaps; but then the majority of winners of the Nobel Prize for Literature are men, so women clearly don't have the monopoly on literary achievement. Men's reserves of testosterone drive us towards success (maybe even in fields like writing), allowing us to use our aggression to achieve even in areas we don't hold the natural advantage. Or is that many of the judges for the Nobel are male?

HUNTERS AND COLLECTORS: MEN AS 'DIFFICULT READERS'

As biology has undoubtedly played a part in determining our social development as well as the form and function of our bodies, evolution is possibly another significant explanation for behavioural differences between the sexes. For hundreds of millennia at the very least, men's fundamental role was that of the hunter. Men's excellent hand-eye co-ordination skills (remember how girls can't throw?), size, strength and sharp spatial awareness of the relationships between objects made men superior to women as hunters of large game. The most successful hunters would have lived longer than their contemporaries, passing on the genes that gave them advantages in the first place – good eyesight for example. Evolution is cumulative, building each generation's successful survival characteristics onto increasingly solid ground. Such powerful genetic heritage is not going to fade away after a few decades of social conditioning from the more diverse activities and attitudes we've adopted comparatively recently. The masculine inclination towards hunting has instead transmuted into other activities – sports, hobbies, being competitive – all of which have kept our target-seeking attitude alive. For example, men's predatory tendency revealed when we consider shopping: market researchers have discovered that men are more likely to 'stalk', seeking out specific items, while women will 'gather', browsing for whatever takes their fancy. Just as our forefathers proved their value to their tribe by claiming and displaying trophies of the kill, men today deal with their subconscious hunter by becoming the proudest of collectors and curators, often winning respect from their fellows based on the size their personal archives, the quality of their contents and their detailed knowledge of their showpieces. We men have sublimated our hunting urge, instead becoming steam-fixated trainspotters, military gamers concerned with precise historical accuracy and mental cataloguers of mind-numbingly tedious yet none-theless fascinating football statistics. Consequently, when it comes to books – expert dealers and second-hand booksellers will confirm this – it is no surprise that the vast majority of serious book collectors (and by this we mean people obsessed with first printings, variant dust jackets and exclusive editions) are men. Our hunger for trophies has made us the most committed of bibliophiles, willing to pay extra for specially bound, signed, limitation-numbered volumes, something publishers are wise to take advantage of when marketing both cult and popular authors; it is no accident that the majority of small presses producing titles for the collector's market specialise in fields popular with men such as hardboiled crime, science fiction and horror.

Collector's editions aside, it could be argued that men have been poorly catered for by the book industry in recent times. There's a widely held view that men generally don't read books: or, to be more accurate, there is a common perception that the majority of men spend far less time reading than do most women, being content to merely chug cans of Stella and stuff themselves with Pringles while watching the FA cup final in high definition on their new fifty-inch widescreen telly. However, in 2002, *The Daily Telegraph* reached the opposite conclusion, stating that if newspapers and electronic media were included, men actually read *more* than women. Yet any examination of reading habits that only includes novels will show women storming ahead. Are we to conclude that men find novels frivolous – that we forsake the lessons that can be learned from invented characters and situations in favour of hard facts?

A smaller interest in fiction amongst men partially explains why publishers might regard the male market as being more difficult to exploit than the female. An article in a 2006 issue of *The Bookseller* magazine focused on 'brand name' best-selling authors like Tom Clancy or Bernard Cornwell as being the key to the male market, inadvertently highlighting the fact that there may be too much reliance upon the old chestnuts of nostalgia (ripping yarns of the Edwardian era that are sometimes a little un-PC), high adventure (chunky techno-thrillers and the likes of Wilbur Smith) and military hard men with guns. While it is relatively easy to establish new genres to engage female readers (the Yummy Mummy novel is a recent example of this), clearly men are thought to be more elusive. Aside from the tendency to read proportionally fewer novels than women, we're inclined to be more obsessive about our hobbies. Men with specific interests are sometimes unable to find titles they would like to leaf through due to the economics of bookselling for while online booksellers who only have to rent relatively cheap warehouses to stock myriads of titles on subjects like militaria and railways, bookshops with expensive high street rents cannot afford to stock deep ranges of slow-selling subjects anymore, so the male reader with specific interests is poorly served.

Also, specialist areas of publishing that often appeal to men are niches by definition, producing few bestsellers, making them commercially challenging to publish, stock and advertise. So you can't blame publishers for finding easier ways to make money, like celebrity autobiographies actually penned by ghostwriters, misery memoirs of childhood abuse that appeal to sentimentally inclined grandmothers and Chick Lit for shopping-fixated sisters. Such tomes are easily marketable through gossipy mags like ***Heat*** or ***Hello***, which tend not to be on the reading list of most males. But opportunities to reach a larger male readership are missed by publishers' marketing teams all the time, especially in the realms of literary fiction – witness **››** Cormac McCarthy's ***The Road***, which could have been additionally advertised as both a science fiction novel (bringing him a whole new readership from a genre fanbase composed almost entirely of men) and as the greatest chronicle of fatherhood published in recent years. Luckily, McCarthy's reputation is already established, but how many superb novels men would love remain unsold due to unimaginative marketing?

Men are sometimes inadvertently excluded from the world of reading by other forces besides possible failings in publisher marketing. The recent growth in the number of reading groups hasn't helped much, as these gatherings tend almost entirely to comprise female members, who much of the time select books by women to discuss at their meetings. If a man wants to join a reading group, his chances of getting the kind of titles we describe in this volume adopted as next month's choice is close to zero. There are also institutions such as the Orange Prize for Fiction, one of Britain's biggest literary awards, which is for female writers only. You can bet your bottom dollar that if there were an equivalent male prize, it would be branded sexist, even though most men (including these authors) aren't bothered by exclusivity of the kind the Orange Prize typifies (although the perceived need for such a prize may be seen as an insult to women writers who have been more than capable of holding their own as literary giants for centuries). In publishing, there are a presses exclusively dedicated to works by female authors – Virago and Women's Press are just two UK imprints that are examples of this kind of feminist publishing (although the former once published seminal classics on equality by H.G. Wells and George Bernard Shaw). There are no publishing imprints that are all-male as a matter of policy, with the exception of some that compete only for the Pink Pound. Sometimes even bookshops drop the ball too, their marketing teams focusing only on Father's Day as the sole opportunity they recognise to get books bought exclusively for men, when a Books For Chaps display would probably go down a storm.

Perhaps it is just the fallout of the feminist revolution and the equality-balancing social policies it has partially sparked over the last few decades that has affected the ability of the book trade, the media and educators to effectively promote reading for men. Wider respect for women's importance in society has long been overdue even in the literate West, so maybe we guys shouldn't complain. Of late, the book trade has started to remember that men often want something a little unreconstructed, well-crafted and perhaps a bit primal, largely due to the success of ***The Dangerous Book For Boys*** (2006). Yet the massive commercial success and positive public response to this admirable book has not yet been properly acted upon in the form of a publishing renaissance in the 'difficult' male market. Our feeling is that male readers are hungry for more than merely reheated nostalgia and mass cloning of Conn and Hal Iggulden's entertaining volume: men don't want slavish imitation, but guidance towards other works they can enjoy, which is why we wrote this book.

IT'S A MAN'S WORD: A BRIEF HISTORY OF BOOKS FOR MEN

Taking a longer view, male readers have generally been catered for handsomely, for there have long been writers, publishers and booksellers only too aware of men's passion for reading. From the dawn of literature itself – myths and folk tales – stories of adventure, heroism, conflict and comradeship have been told to entrance men. Greek and Roman classics from Homer to Tacitus, British doomfests like ***Beowulf*** (c. 700–750 AD), Scandanavian sagas such as ***The Kalevala***, Middle Eastern masterpieces like ***The Epic of Gilgamesh*** (c. 2000 BC) and Asian edifices like ***Monkey*** (c. 1590) are all packed with action, excitement and moral dilemmas that still appeal today. The medieval chivalric romances – tales of old when knights were bold that fathered the modern novel – not only catered for ladies who dreamt of being swept off their feet by handsome chaps in shining armour, but inspired men to seek glory in arms or at least experience the pleasures of an honourable martial existence by proxy. The often unrealistically gallant heroes of these tales were challenged in the sixteenth century by the protagonists of Spanish Picaresque novels like ***Lazarillo De Tormes*** (1554). These lovable rogues whose low breeding, episodic japery and earthy humour confirm them not only as the latter-day equivalents of today's literary wideboy figures but also as harbingers of the school of Realism. In ***Don Quixote*** (1604), Cervantes arguably created the modern novel by parodying the chivalric romances while using the technique of the Picaresque, encouraging men to recognise and mock their own illusions while building a new psychological self-awareness into the ancient quest narrative that still acts as the skeleton of major popular fiction genres such as fantasy, encouraging readers to see the metaphor as part of the surface of a narrative, not just its moral heart.

But the Romantics didn't take the Picaresque lying down. By the late eighteenth century leading writers from all over Europe – most of them male – were tackling the big issues of freedom, the sublime and the new currents in thought inspired by Enlightenment politics and science. Poets, dramatists and novelists all created monumental male protagonists, some heroic, some villainous, most of them fascinatingly ambiguous and occasionally amoral. From Byron's ***Don Juan*** (unfinished at 1824) to Schiller's ***The Robbers*** (1781), from Goethe's ***The Sorrows of Young Werther*** (1774) to Rousseau's ***Julie*** (1761) (where a free-loving female anti-hero gets in on the rebellion act), the Romantics inspired generations of courageous chaps to cast off the shackles of the repressive Middle Ages and embrace the new world opening up before them. Gothic novelists represented the extreme end of Romanticism, with authors like Matthew Lewis and William Beckford revelling in the evil of their licentious characters. The French Revolution also encouraged the extremes of pornography to pour from the pen of the Marquis De Sade, whose ***120 Days of Sodom*** (1785), although uncompleted, remains the pinnacle of depravity even in the age of internet porn. Healthier perhaps was Henry Fielding's rollicking ***Tom Jones*** (1749), which had been preceded by Clelland's ***Fanny Hill*** (1748), but pornography really came into its own in Victorian England, with periodicals such as ***The Pearl*** displaying fascination with the deflowering of servant-girl virgins and flagellation. Victorian erotica is still reprinted today, anonymous titles such as ***Astrid Cane*** (late nineteenth century) reappearing every now and then in small press editions.

Publishers hadn't always relied upon fiction to win male customers, of course. The age of exploration had diverted readers eager for sensation and encouraged numerous young men to take to the ocean. Unreliable travel memoirs had existed for millennia, but the age of sail brought opportunities to mariners with a literary bent. Dana, Melville and Darwin speak to us fundamentally through narratives of their voyages, pioneering not just travel writing but laying the groundwork for the naval adventure novel. This genre also enlivened the modern war novel and the techno-thriller, with authors like Douglas Reeman and Clive Cussler applying new military technology to classic adventure storytelling.

With exploration came colonisation and by the time the New World was being settled, emigrants to North America found they needed new literary voices to explore their new freedoms from European rule, the realities of the frontier and the moral complexities that arose from their habitation of a new continent that had long been occupied. Most of the pioneers of American literature's early days were men writing for a male audience. James Fennimore Cooper is often hailed as the precursor of the Western, while the mixture of traditional European seriousness and strange narrative novelties and psychological twists found in the work of Charles Brockden Brown (the first US writer to make his living solely as an author) pointed toward a questioning of reality we see today in writers like Philip K. Dick, **››** Paul Auster and **››** Brett Easton Ellis, who all command largely male readerships.

Once the industrial age gathered pace, British writers became obsessed with the novel of character and social niceties: the legacy of

Jane Austen coloured the English novel, while authors of a more revolutionary caste like Robert Bage (whose 1796 novel ***Hermsprong*** sets the refreshing freethinking approach of the European and US enlightenment novelists against the stuffiness of English hypocrisy) lay forgotten. But the Victorian era nevertheless offered ample literary inspiration for writers more focused on ideas than tearoom etiquette – while Dickens injected the grotesque and memorable into the livid tapestries of his social commentaries and introduced the word detective into the English language (thereby laying a claim as a pioneer of crime fiction), the expansion of the Empire helped codify the spirit of confidence, discipline and stiff upper lip that characterised popular writers like Kipling, Conan Doyle and Buchan. The values of writers like these – whose glory days were the times when much of the map was pink – are the basis of the wave of nostalgia publishing we've seen recently. Meanwhile, Edgar Allen Poe and Jules Verne looked to the future and worked on developing science fiction, some of whose roots lay in travellers' tales and adventure stories.

Magazines had long been a source of popular fiction in both Europe and the USA: periodicals such as the UK's ***Blackwood's*** (1817–32) not only published criticism and political commentary, but showcased short stories, allowing forms like the ghost/horror story to find a market and develop. Such magazines were the foundation of many of today's popular genres – during the nineteenth century, novels were serialised in newspapers, while short stories and novellettes were published as chapbook 'dime novels' (in the USA) and 'penny dreadfuls' (in the UK), these bargain basement formats eventually metamorphosing into the pulp magazines of the first half of the twentieth century. Western tales were the staple of the dime novels throughout the frontier period, sensational retellings of real events so fictionalised that it is nearly impossible for historians to separate truth from fantasy in many cases, popular cowboy pulps later emerging from this tradition of embellished accounts of real gunfights. In the first half of the twentieth century, writers of ambition started tackling Westerns, turning out some classic works that inspired many of the more celebrated Hollywood cowboy movies many of us guys still thrill to. Even today, nothing empties the TV lounge of women like a classic Western on DVD and few female writers have ever successfully tackled the genre.

Fantasy and horror stories had lain at the roots of narrative from the dawn of language and can be found in all cultures, suggesting that such tales are the most protean of all types of fiction, but they really came into their own in the Gothic period. Ghost and vampire stories (usually featuring male monsters, manly heroes and swooning, toothsome female victims) naturally appealed to men and the majority of such tales published before the twentieth century were by men. Today, the domain of the undead bloodsucker seems to have been claimed by females, but the majority of non-vampire horrors are still penned (and purchased) by men. The contemporary fantasy novel (fundamentally comprising the sword-and-sorcery tale of the kind popularised by Tolkien), although originating in those Medieval romances, was recreated by Pre-Raphaelite types such as William Morris, though the real father of today's interminable trilogies is ›› Robert E. Howard. Few women (apart from trailblazers like Leigh Brackett and C.L. Moore) published sword and sorcery until the field boomed in the 1970s, blood-and-thunder merchants such as Fritz Leiber, Poul Anderson and Michael Moorcock setting the standards of barbarian swashbuckling in the 1950s and 1960s. These yarns of destiny, death and damnation found little favour amongst female readers, but today many young women have been converted to fantasy by the likes of Ursula K. LeGuin, who has arguably brought greater emotional depth to magic and blade-yielding.

By the early twentieth century the age of the pulp magazines was dawning, their impact upon contemporary reading tastes too often ignored by critics. Aside from Modernism, the most important development in twentieth-century literature was undoubtedly the codifying of various hugely popular genres: the crime novel, science fiction, fantasy, horror, the spy thriller and the maritime adventure all became formularised professionally by influential editors who paid magazine writers by the word. While this sounds like a bad thing, it ensured that talented authors of humble background had an inroad into literary careers. The giants of the pulps were Edgar Rice Burroughs, H.P. Lovecraft, Raymond Chandler and Dashiel Hammett. The golden age of the pulps was over by 1960, flourishing alongside the flowering of television, the talkies and radio. Like these competing technologies, genre fiction began to dominate mass-market publishing, especially once paperbacks made their appearance. Although the first truly successful paperback imprint (Penguin) launched in 1935, it wasn't until the late fifties that paperbacks really took off and fiction magazines went into decline.

Penguin became infamous in 1960 for publishing D.H. Lawrence's ***Lady Chatterly's Lover*** (1928). The resultant obscenity trial was the first of several that marked literature's emergence from censorship in the sixties. Maurice Girodias' Olympia Press is the most notable house of recent times to issue books to be read with one hand; the distinctive green paperbacks in the Traveller's Companion series. Confiscated from tourists regularly at UK customs throughout the fifties, Olympia published low filth and high art (the former often written under pseudonyms by the authors of the latter) from the likes of ›› William S. Burroughs, ›› Henry Miller and ›› Alexander Trocchi. Such printing activities often led to obscenity cases, 'banned books' and much publicity, things that appealed to a free-thinking (and a sometimes prurient) male audience in particular. Novels featuring homosexuality, like ›› Hubert Selby's ***Last Exit To Brooklyn*** (1957), were also subject to precedent-setting legal cases, causing many to recall the shameful punishment inflicted upon Oscar Wilde decades before. Even in today's liberated climate publishers can end up in trouble – British house Savoy Books (we recommend their publication ***The Gas*** (1970), a sexy SF novel by Charles Platt) got into trouble with the police in the 1980s over some taboo-shattering satirical adult comics.

Comics have always been frowned upon of course, one reason why we boys love them. Originating at the end of the nineteenth century, their definitive form – the Superhero saga – emerged with the first appearance of Superman in ***Action Comics #1*** (1938). The Batman appeared in 1939, making DC Comics the undisputed masters of pictorial storytelling throughout what fans call the Golden Age until Marvel brought new depths to the field with Stan Lee and Jack Kirby's ***Fantastic Four #1*** (1961), ushering in the Silver Age, generally regarded as the most vital period in the history of comics. By the mid eighties, the Sunday supplements started getting excited about the seriousness of the contemporary 'graphic novel' as titles like ***Watchmen*** (collected 1987) and ***Batman: The Dark Night Returns*** (1986) sold in their tens of thousands, while (often baldly autobiographical) underground comics rising from the hippy counterculture were an established subgenre by the late sixties. The last genre to become reasonably respectable, graphic fiction enjoys an audience that is still largely masculine.

So for contemporary man, there is a whole world of literature published over the centuries for men to discover and enjoy. We hope this book will help men everywhere embark on the next stage of their journey into reading, as although this may not be a man's world any longer, once you open books by our chosen authors, you'll find that at least a man's *word* still carries plenty of weight.

A–Z LIST OF ENTRIES BY AUTHOR

The following is a checklist of authors and titles featured in this book.

Kingsley Amis	*The Green Man*
Lance Armstrong	*It's Not About The Bike*
A.A. Attanasio	*Wyvern*
Paul Auster	*The Music of Chance*
J.G. Ballard	*Crash*
George Bataille	*The Story of the Eye*
Brendan Behan	*Borstal Boy*
Saul Bellow	*The Adventures of Augie Marsh*
Patrick Bishop	*Fighter Boys*
Kyril Bonfiglioli	*Don't Point That Thing At Me*
Martin Booth	*A Magick Life*
Mark Bowden	*Black Hawk Down*
Chester Brown	*The Playboy*
Charles Bukowski	*Post Office*
Edward Bunker	*No Beast So Fierce*
James Lee Burke	*Lay Down My Sword and Shield*
William S. Burroughs	*Junkie*
Dino Buzzati	*The Tartar Steppe*
Deborah Cadbury	*Space Race*
James M. Cain	*The Postman Always Rings Twice*

Carlos Castaneda	*The Teachings of Don Juan*
Walter Van Tilburg Clark	*The Ox-Bow Incident*
Jeremy Clarkson	*You Know You Got Soul*
Jonathan Coe	*The Rotter's Club*
Douglas Coupland	*Generation X*
James Crumley	*One to Count Cadence*
Miles Davis	*Miles*
Len Deighton	*The Ipcress File*
Isabelle Eberhardt	*The Oblivion Seekers*
Brett Easton Ellis	*American Psycho*
Mick Farren	*The Tale of Willy's Rats*
Ian Fleming	*You Only Live Twice*
George MacDonald Fraser	*Flashman*
Alasdair Gray	*1982 Janine*
Graham Greene	*The Ministry of Fear*
Stephen Gregory	*The Cormorant*
Ernesto 'Che' Guevara	*The Motorcycle Diaries*
Ben Hamper	*Rivethead*
M. John Harrison	*Climbers*
Ernest Hemingway	*Islands in the Stream*
Herman Hesse	*Steppenwolf*
Patricia Highsmith	*Ripley Under Ground*
Anthony Hope	*The Prisoner of Zenda*
Robert E. Howard	*The Complete Chronicles of Conan*
Simon Hughes	*A Lot of Hard Yakka*
J.K. Husymans	*Against Nature*
M.R. James	*Casting The Runes and Other Ghost Stories*
Garry Kilworth	*Witchwater County*

John Rechy	*City of Night*
Luke Rhinehart	*The Dice Man*
Graham Robb	*Rimbaud*
Philip Roth	*Portnoy's Complaint*
Leopold Von Sacher-Masoch	*Venus In Furs*
J.D. Salinger	*The Catcher in the Rye*
James Salter	*The Hunters*
Robert Falcon Scott	*Journals*
Hubert Selby Jnr.	*The Demon*
Will Self	*The Book of Dave*
Robert Silverberg	*The Book of Skulls*
Dan Simmons	*The Song of Kali*
Joe Simpson	*Touching the Void*
Iceberg Slim	*Pimp*
Richard Stark	*Slayground*
Danny Sugerman	*Wonderland Avenue*
Hunter S. Thompson	*Fear and Loathing in Las Vegas*
Peter Tinniswood	*A Touch of Daniel*
Alex Trocchi	*Young Adam*
Charles Willeford	*Cockfighter*
Colin Wilson	*Ritual in the Dark*
Tom Wolfe	*Bonfire of the Vanities*
Tobias Wolff	*Old School*
Clive Woodward	*Winning*

A–Z OF ENTRIES

KINGSLEY AMIS (1922–95) UK

THE GREEN MAN (1970)

Maurice, the womanising, alcoholic proprietor of The Green Man inn comes across a woman on his upstairs landing, only for her to vanish inexplicably – but then he is prone to hallucinations and it's not as if the pub has a haunted history – not since Victorian times that is. A second encounter with the auburn-tressed visitant is followed by a sighting of what Maurice is convinced must be the ghost of infernal eighteenth century conjuror Dr Thomas Underhill. Thus prompted into some research, Maurice decides on an attempt to contact this second, tempestuous spirit. Finding it hard enough to communicate with the real world, however, Maurice's priorities are messily divided between discovering the facts behind other local supernatural traditions and instilling in the doctor's wife the idea that a *ménage a trois* might be rather good fun.

Oxford graduate Amis was best known for his satirical novels that target various segments of British society. He debunked the pretension of university life to brilliant effect in ***Lucky Jim***, and uproariously sent up the Welsh middle classes in Booker Prize winning ***The Old Devils***. Yet much of Amis' most memorable work was that which experimented with genre fiction, for example, the sozzled landlord's desire to cram in as much illicit pleasure as possible is put into perspective by discussions of mortality brought on by the spectral manifestations, Amis managing to inject intelligent humour into this deftly-crafted horror story.

Amis was a renowned boozer himself and there is a longstanding debate (supported by anecdotal evidence these authors have encountered) as to whether his drinking habits approximated those of Maurice in *The Green Man*. Sexuality and conjugal freedom are also subjects that frequently feature in his books, and his own marriage broke down after an affair with writer Elizabeth Jane Howard. His son Martin is, of course, also popular with male readers, himself a hugely successful writer of blackly humorous novels (often with controversial subject matter) such as *Dead Babies* and *Time's Arrow*.

TV series: *The Green Man* (1990)

Read on

The Alteration; *Colonel Sun* (written as Robert Markham, the first officially-sanctioned Bond novel published after » Ian Fleming's death).
Fear: Robert Aickman, *Sub Rosa*; H.P. Lovecraft, *The Dunwich Horror and Others*; Algernon Blackwood, *Ancient Sorceries*

LANCE ARMSTRONG (b. 1971) (with SALLY JENKINS)

USA

IT'S NOT ABOUT THE BIKE (2000) (NF)

There comes a time in every man's life when he realises he is not indestructible, when he stops laughing off prolonged colds and unidentified lumps, and begins to imagine the worst when illness strikes. Cyclist Lance Armstrong was only twenty-four and still feeling utterly immortal when he was diagnosed with a cancer that spread rapidly from his testicles to his brain. It is not so much his courage in defying the odds, returning to health and getting back on his bike that mark him as unique. It is the fact that before he fell ill, he was a promising athlete unknown outside his sport and afterwards won seven straight Tours de France: a feat which sets him apart from anyone else in his field irrespective of what he had to overcome.

The title of the book, although obviously in part a reference to Armstrong's battle with disease, relates to the fact that bicycling at the highest level is a physical, mental and moral test. These disciplines may have been factors in his survival but he is smart enough to recognise that fighters often die and those who resign themselves to death often survive. Insisting that he was lucky, Armstrong nevertheless remains an inspirational figure as well as perhaps *the* ultimate athlete. Proposing this opens up a debate on whether partaking in contact sport or being an all-rounder are prerequisites to being considered the greatest. Armstrong confesses to having poor hand-eye coordination, therefore failing at ball games but it's difficult to see past the man who won consistently in an arena which is not only exceptionally tough and unforgiving but also historically bigoted against non-Europeans.

While Armstrong's descriptions of symptoms and medical procedures may well make you queasy, the tale of a blokeish Texan tearaway colliding head-on with his own mortality and becoming stronger, infinitely more mature and massively successful as a result will leave you happily gasping for breath.

Sequels: *Every Second Counts* (NF); *The Lance Armstrong Performance Program* (with Chris Carmichael) (NF)

Read on

Paul Kimmage, ***Rough Ride*** (NF); John Diamond, ***C*** (NF); Helen Rollason, *Life's Too Short* (NF)

A.A. ATTANASIO (b. 1951) USA

WYVERN (1988)

Son of a Dutch merchant seaman and a native girl, Jaki Gefjon is born in Borneo in the early seventeenth century. Growing up in the dense rainforest with his mother, blonde, tawny-skinned Gefjon is shunned by local tribes. Schooled in sorcery by soul-catcher Jabalwan, the boy's magical jungle initiation is interrupted when he is kidnapped by pirates. Almost immediately rescued by the crew of a larger freebooting ship, Gefjon swears loyalty to Trevor Pym, one-eyed captain of the sleek vessel. Framed for piracy as a callow youth by the villainous Quarle, Pym had little chance of proving his innocence. Instead, he bears the brand of a privateer proudly, scourging the seas of south-east Asia covertly, his ship only unfurling the flag of plunder when Pym's chosen victim cannot escape. The standard Pym flies is no ordinary Jolly Roger, but the rampant image of a Wyvern, a legendary dragon which symbolises the very life-force itself. Gefjon is set on leading a reckless existence, identifying passionately with the draconian banner. When he encounters Lucinda Quarle, grand-daughter of Pym's betrayer, Gefjon seizes the grail of destiny and drains the cup to its dregs.

As boys we all play at being black-hearted sea-dogs, our childhood imagination captured by chronicles of cutlasses and treasure-chests. While history books have revealed the truth about privateers, we still prefer the romantic side of the buccaneer legend presented in *Treasure Island*. *Wyvern* is a sprawling epic that fulfils the expectations Stevenson's classic instilled in us, its archetypal elements enlivened by the heady dose of mysticism Attanasio pours into the mix, which its publishers likened to that of ›› Castaneda. The tropical lushness of Attanasio's multi-hued yet poised prose is in exemplary harmony with his pulse-pounding subject matter, his expertise with his driven cast ideally suited to this blockbuster tale of love, vengeance and transcendence. Marrying colourful escapism with sensual and angular poetic writing, Attanasio has written SF, fantasy and Arthurian sagas. *Wyvern* is his best-balanced book and easily the finest pirate novel of modern times. A cult book rather than a bestseller, *Wyvern* appeared at the same time as Tim Power's zombie pirate story *On Stranger Tides*, when freebooters were temporarily unfashionable.

Read on

Radix

Treasure and treachery: Marcus Clarke, *His Natural Life*; Jon E. Lewis (ed.) *The Mammoth Book of Pirates*; Robert Nye, *Voyage of the Destiny*; John Steinbeck, *Cup of Gold*

PAUL AUSTER (b. 1947) USA

THE MUSIC OF CHANCE (1990)

After his wife walks out on him, Boston fire fighter Nashe finds that his life is disintegrating. Working shifts to pay off medical care debts incurred by his dead mother, Nashe is forced to place his two-year-old daughter with his sister in Minnesota. Out of the blue Nashe is contacted by a lawyer: the father he has not seen for thirty years has died of cancer and left him $200,000. With no anchor of responsibility to tether him to his past existence, Nashe pays his creditors, sets up a trust fund for his child, buys a sports car and drives away from everything, relishing the empty freedom and calm solitude of the open roads.

Nashe has been aimlessly traversing the highways of America for thirteen months when he impulsively stops to offer help to a ragged little weasel of a man. Jack Pozzi is a professional gambler down on his luck. Intrigued by Pozzi's patter and in need of company, Nashe checks them into a hotel where the former demonstrates his impressive skills at cards. Dismayed by the fact that he will have to cancel an important game he had scheduled with two wealthy eccentrics, Pozzi is delighted when Nashe offers to come in as Jack's betting partner and put up the necessary stake money. But when the drifting duo sit at the rich men's gaming table after a surreal tour of their shared estate, they find that lady luck sometimes plays the wildest hand of all.

Paul Auster burst upon the literary scene to enormous acclaim with his bestselling ***New York Trilogy*** (collected 1987). His elegant prose and obsession with the random wanderings of existentially challenged protagonists has won him a massive following, especially amongst men, who are drawn to the complimentary qualities of distance and mystery Auster is effortlessly adept at conjuring. Seasoned with unobtrusive literary allusions and fascinating narrative twists that reflect the contingency of everyday life, Auster's novels work equally well as art and entertainment. ***The Music of Chance*** speaks eloquently of accountability, man's need for freedom and the seductive perils of gambling while being an excellent introduction to the addictive works of this stunning, original writer.

Film version: *The Music of Chance* (1993)

Read on

Moon Palace; ***Leviathan***; ***The Book of Illusion***; ***Brooklyn Follies***; ***The Invention of Solitude*** (NF, covering the author's relationship with his distant father)

J.G. BALLARD (b. 1930) b. China, UK

CRASH (1973)

Recuperating in hospital after a motorway smash which killed the other driver involved, James Ballard encounters Vaughan, an amoral scientist obsessed with the sexual implications of car crashes and their devastating effects upon their victims. Instead of being repelled by Vaughan's fixations, Ballard finds his own attitude towards automobile accidents has become eroticised too, using cars as the venue for his cold carnal trysts with his wife Catherine and Helen Remington, the widow of the man who died on Ballard's own bonnet.

Behind the wheel Ballard haunts overpasses and slipways with

Vaughan, abusing whores and dropping acid at maximum acceleration. The men imagine spectacular collisions, craving sculptures of twisted metal and violated flesh, Vaughan seeking his apotheosis in the ideal wedding of sex and technology, longing to die in a textbook crash involving the actress Elizabeth Taylor. Building up to this final, gloriously hideous orgasm, Vaughan performs a series of perilous stunts, re-enacting the vehicular fatalities of celebrities to an audience comprising an underground subculture of accident survivors. All of this is presented to the reader in an unnervingly matter-of-fact tone, the author even using his own name for the narrator.

We're all aware of the notion of car as penis substitute, seeing this in action daily as we drive to work. *Crash* exposes the psychological expression of our worship of fast cars, expressing fearlessly the libidinous energies sublimated in motoring culture. An eloquent pornographic novel that also prevails as high calibre literature, *Crash* is a shocking, profoundly original triumph of the contemporary imagination and a hymn to the machine that is the primary icon of affluent western lifestyles. After reading it, watching *Top Gear* never seems the same again.

J.G. Ballard's childhood experiences in World War II inspired the equally renowned *Empire of the Sun* (1984) and the dystopian SF (which examines the impact of technology on human consciousness) that typifies his opus. One chilling piece of not insignificant trivia is that the author was involved in a serious car accident soon after finishing *Crash*. Luckily for us, he survived to write another day.

Film version: *Crash* (1996)
Thematic sequels: *Concrete Island, High Rise*

Read on

The Terminal Beach

V. Vale (ed) *J.G. Ballard: Conversations* (NF); *J.G. Ballard: Interviews* (NF)

GEORGES BATAILLE (1897–1962) France

STORY OF THE EYE (1928, revised 1940)

Originally published pseudonymously, *Story of the Eye* was the first novel by surrealist Georges Bataille. A graphic sexual chronicle – pornographic, certainly, it is also a breaking down of artistic expectations, a kind of anti-literature that Sartre saw as a post-religious classic. But never mind all that: Bataille's book is a tale of erotic exploration which will prompt male readers to recall their own sexual awakenings, although the narrator's exploits easily trump the tame and timid deeds of most normal folk, whose eyes have supposedly been neutered so that they are unable to appreciate wild, debauched, filthy pleasures. During one orgiastic gathering where bodily fluids of all kinds mingle in a flood of decadence, pious but impressionable Marcelle is driven insane by what she sees while the youthful hero flees the scene to avoid parental censure. A dreamlike quality shrouds the narrative as he and his loose-bladdered lover Simone enter a new phase of perversity but, without reticent Marcelle as their foil, their sexual encounters are unsatisfactory. A morbid longing leads them to the walls of her sanatorium, but who will benefit from her release and who will suffer?

As much as it is a surrealist dreamscape replete with occular/egg/testicle imagery and urine, ***Story of the Eye*** is about breaking the rules and doing what comes naturally, ignoring romantic constraints in search of fulfilment. But sex between Simone and the narrator is not just pleasure: it is obsession, it is pain, it is close to death. Eyes are a recurring surrealist motif from Bealu to Dali (this author will never forget the razorblade slicing an eyeball in Dali and Bunuel's short film, ***Un Chien Andalou***, which he saw at a tender age whilst staying with a French family) and Bataille was a key figure in this movement which crossed all artistic media as well as influencing modern thinkers such as Foucault and Derrida.

Read on

Blue of Noon; *The Accursed Share* (NF)

Marcel Bealu, *The Experience of the Night*; Andre Breton, *Nadja*; Pauline Reage, *The Story of O*

READONATHEME: PAINTER MAN

The male artist: irreverent wit, sexual outrageousness, elemental creativity, cosmic angst

Salvador Dali, *The Secret Life of Salvador Dali* (NF), *Diary of a Madman* (NF), *The Unspeakable Confessions of Salvador Dali* (NF)

Eugene Delacroix, *The Journal* (NF)

Giorgio De Chirico, *Hebdemeros*

Gilbert and George, *The Words of Gilbert and George* (NF)
Brion Gysin, *The Process*
Steven Naifeh and Gregory White, *Jackson Pollock: An American Saga* (NF)
David Sylvester, *Interviews with Francis Bacon*; *The Brutality of Fact* (NF)
Vincent Van Gogh, *The Letters* (NF)
Andy Warhol, *From A to B and Back Again: The Philosophy of Andy Warhol* (NF)
Patrick White, *The Vivesector*

BRENDAN BEHAN (1923–64) Ireland

BORSTAL BOY (1958) (NF)

Fledgling teenage IRA bomber Behan has his own opinions on how to achieve freedom for Ireland, but when he is caught with a cache of explosives his personal liberty draws to an abrupt halt. Despised by local police, he consoles himself with the certainty that attempting to blow up a shipyard is acceptable in the face of English acts of oppression, and consistent with the image of a romantic hero. Time spent waiting to be convicted is brought to grim life: the smell of soap and excrement, the bleak and doleful days, but also the colourful relationships with inmates and officials. Like all terrorists, he has brushed up on the historical facts that best serve his arguments and he is not shy in quarrelling with guards and priests. Borstal itself has a boarding school feel to it except that there is outdoor labour and nobody gets suspended for smoking. Fistfights and punishments abound, but there is also personal enrichment through friendship, religious observance and literature.

Ultimately the prisoner emerges as a more tolerant young man who understands the feelings of his traditional enemies, eventually abhorring the sectarian violence that shaped his early character. Behan was an adult when he wrote ***Borstal Boy*** so it is impossible to say whether he endowed his younger self with greater wit, maturity and philosophical consciousness than he actually possessed. Nevertheless, the book's hero is an amiable, feisty fellow, versed in flattery and the psychology of getting by in a young offender's institution, and his tale is told with warmth and apparent integrity.

Behan came from a family of radical republicans and was heavily influenced by his mother who numbered Michael Collins amongst her friends. A writer of plays, poetry and pornography, he is considered one of Ireland's great literary figures. A serious drinker from childhood onwards and alcohol, combined with diabetes, led to an early and somewhat ignominious death that for a time negated the respect earned by his literary output.

Read on

The Quare Fellow; ***The Hostage*** (both drama)
Peter Taylor, ***The Provos*** (NF); Eamon Collins, ***Killing Rage*** (NF); Jean Genet, ***Our Lady of the Flowers***

SAUL BELLOW (1915–2005) Canada

THE ADVENTURES OF AUGIE MARCH (1953)

Martin Amis once said that this book is the great American novel, which is rather like claiming that Bellow had captured the extinct Great Auk. A magnificent epic of the everyday, the novel follows March through the many professions he samples in his quest for 'self' around the time of the Great Depression. Characters who would grace the works of Dickens or Zola coast through the narrative: at one time Augie cares for a penny-pinching, wheelchair-bound tycoon; at another he is shipwrecked with a mad genius.

Schooled in deception as a young boy by his Grandma Lausch, infected but stifled by his brother Simon's heroic convictions and lust for money, March discovers that the world is full of lies and liars, and it is no surprise when he falls in with gangsters (an experience Bellow also encountered). Nevertheless, whether encountering severe poverty, extreme wealth or outright criminality, Augie has a young man's burgeoning philosophical appreciation for all accrued experience, and everything serves to expand his consciousness. The picaresque nature of the book has led some critics to compare it to ***Don Quixote***, but there is also something of the feel of ***On The Road*** (written two years earlier from the dope-and-poetry perspective of the Beat Generation but actually a much blander take on the voyage of self-discovery).

Bellow was born Solomon Bellows of Russian-Jewish stock, moving to Chicago early in life. He studied anthropology, a subject that, as evidenced by many references in his books, continued to interest him in later life. He won the Nobel Prize in 1976 and used his acceptance speech to call for an intellectual awakening amongst authors. In 1967, he served as a war correspondent in the Arab–Israeli conflict.

Bellow deserves a wider readership but suffers from the fact that, by dint of their titles and stuffy jackets, his novels seem to promise tedium. What they actually deliver is hypnotising characters and some of the best writing of the past century.

Read on

Humboldt's Gift; *The Victim*

Jewish experience: *To Jerusalem and Back* (NF); Theodore Dreiser, *An American Tragedy*; Emile Zola, *The Masterpiece* (aka *His Masterpiece*)

READONATHEME: NOBEL MAN

The Nobel Prize for Literature was first awarded in 1901. Jean Paul Sartre (1905–80, France) – philosopher, critic and resistance fighter – famously refused the Nobel when it was offered him. His novel *Nausea* remains the ideal companion to Camus' *The Outsider*. Here are some other recommended titles by some of the numerous male winners.

Ivo Andric, *The Bosnian Chronicle*
Samuel Beckett, *The Beckett Trilogy*
Elias Canetti, *Crowds and Power* (NF)
Winston Churchill, *My Early Life* (NF)
Andre Gide, *The Immoralist*

William Golding, *Lord of the Flies*
Gunter Grass, *The Tin Drum*
Knut Hamsun, *Growth of the Soil*
›› Ernest Hemingway, *The Snows of Kilimanjaro*
›› Herman Hesse, *Narziss and Goldmund*

PATRICK BISHOP (b. 1952) UK

FIGHTER BOYS (2003) (NF)

Fighter planes were developed as a defensive counterfoil against bombers. In World War II they were used to thwart the Luftwaffe's intention to bring Britain to her knees via a gargantuan aerial assault in the summer of 1940. In his meticulously detailed book, Patrick Bishop supplies some background and history of the RAF, providing a compelling insight into the hurried technological advances in aircraft production during the build-up to war, but his main business is with individuals; the bright-eyed young heroes who might be found downing Messerschmitts in the morning and pints that same afternoon.

Bishop suggests that airmen were as popular as film stars in the thirties and forties. The reader is transported to an age where civilians cheered aviators and (to a certain extent) policy makers, rather than bewailing lost lives and pointless war-mongering as is generally the case today. It was an era where fighting was still seen as a chivalrous, glamorous adventure, and the likelihood of dying was rarely entertained by young volunteers eager to be plunged into the action. Drawn by such romantic notions, aspiring pilots of all social backgrounds came together harmoniously (once predictable snobbery had been brushed away by the evident equal merits of working class recruits) to defend the nation's skies.

Bishop's ability to empathise with his remarkable young subjects is not purely down to research and interviews. In his role as foreign correspondent, he witnessed other conflicts up close, and these experiences have helped to distil the veteran testimonies of 1940. History books relying predominantly on first hand accounts can, perversely, be less convincing than fiction, because we are continually bombarded by often contradictory diary entries and opinions. Bishop's great strength lies in intertwining the protagonists' experiences with the richly described factual material, enlivening the story of ordinary men defending their homeland from invasion. Warning: anyone who has ever considered the selfless heroism and gallantry of our aces in that dark time when Britain was the only country in Europe actively opposing the Axis risks being moved to tears by some of the heartrending incidents retold in this stirring book.

Read on

Bomber Boys (NF); *3 Para* (NF)

Len Deighton, ***Fighter*** (NF); Billy Drake, ***Billy Drake, Fighter Leader*** (NF); Stephen Bungay, ***The Most Dangerous Enemy*** (NF); Derek Robinson, *Goshawk Squadron*

KYRIL BONFIGLIOLI (1928–85) UK

DON'T POINT THAT THING AT ME (1972)

Raffish, villainous but cowardly-at-heart art dealer Charlie Mortdecai is visited by his public school contemporary, Martland, who is investigating the disappearance of a Goya canvas. Mortdecai knows something of the matter but divulges as many lies as truths and is, in any case, unsure as to what much of his information relates to; notably the photograph of faceless men involved in a homosexual act that has been secreted in the National Gallery. Prone to playful language and imaginative threats (given weight by his hired goon, Jock Strapp), Mortdecai ends his encounters variously with electrocuted testicles, a punched-in face and the brains of an acquaintance spattered about him.

Whether being shot at, seduced by the wife of a customer Martland wants him to kill, or shaking off a mysterious blue car that tails his Rolls across America, the boozing fop retains his penchant for cutting *bon mots* (if not his nerve, which fails him regularly). An unforgettable comic anti-hero, Mortdecai traipses through a side-splitting array of bizarre scrapes like a sinister Bertie Wooster.

Don't Point That Thing At Me is the first part of a series of spirited, joyfully written comedies (the first three being collected in a UK omnibus edition as ***The Mortdecai Trilogy***). The self-conscious, rotund and formerly handsome Charlie with his double dealing decadence and very English bumbling is a fabulous creation by an author who playfully protests too much when claiming that there is nothing autobiographical here. Bonfiglioli himself was an art dealer with an epicure's love of the finer things in life who also edited genre fiction magazines. His novels are in part a tribute to and distortion of P.G. Wodehouse's works, containing several overt references to Jeeves and his errant master.

Sequels: *Something Nasty in the Woodshed*; *After You With The Pistol*; *The Great Mortdecai Moustache Mystery*

Read on

All The Tea in China

P.G. Wodehouse, *The Code of the Woosters*

Comic crime: Daniel Pennac, *The Fairy Gunmother*; Andrey Kurkov, *A Matter of Death and Life*

MARTIN BOOTH (1944–2004) UK

A MAGICK LIFE (A BIOGRAPHY OF ALEISTER CROWLEY) (2000) (NF)

The tabloid press once described him as 'The wickedest man in the world'. The Beatles put him on the sleeve of *Sgt. Pepper's* alongside their other idols. Jimmy Page of Led Zeppelin was obsessed with him and collected all the memorabilia associated with the man that he could, including his house. He was a gin enthusiast, poet, world-class mountaineer, drug addict and charlatan. Or was he?

Edward Alexander Crowley (1875–1947) was the son of a wealthy, puritanical family of Victorian brewers and claimed to be the Great Beast 666 of the Bible's Book of Revelation. He was almost certainly the most significant occultist of modern times. Throughout his flamboyant, decadent life, Crowley infiltrated magical orders, formed his own cults, engaged in his own form of ritual 'sex magick' with both genders and attracted numerous acolytes. Although he died just as the Beat Generation was coming into existence, Crowley has a better claim than anyone to being the Grandfather of modern counterculture. His personal maxim (partially lifted from Rabelais) was the immortal proclamation 'Do what Thou wilt shall be the whole of the law: love is the law, love under will.' In this statement the worship of freedom practiced by artists and western youth is encapsulated.

Of all the Crowley biographies we have read, Martin Booth's is by far the best-written and most balanced account. Lucid in its approach and open-minded yet suitably questioning regarding the reality of its subject's supposed command of supernatural forces, Booth wades through the mythology obscuring the man to reveal a portrait of Crowley as close to the facts as we could reasonably expect.

An internationally respected writer who was at home with fiction, biography and general non-fiction, Booth received insufficient praise for this excellent book, possibly due to the arguably vulgar nature of its subject. Despite his undeniably unsavoury character, Crowley nevertheless possessed the infernal courage and breathtaking audacity to defiantly pioneer the 'new age'– consequently, every contemporary man will enjoy learning about this Oliver Reed of Satanists.

Read on

The Great Beasts' novels: *Diary of a Drug Fiend*; *Moonchild*

666 Fiction (characters inspired by Crowley): W. Somerset Maugham, *The Magician*; Dennis Wheatley, *The Devil Rides Out*; ›› Colin Wilson, *Man Without a Shadow* (aka *The Sex Diary of a Metaphysician* aka *The Sex Diary of Gerard Sorme*)

MARK BOWDEN (b. 1951) USA

BLACK HAWK DOWN (1999) (NF)

While the principle of never leaving a man behind in action makes moral sense, it can be hard to reconcile with the resultant, additional loss of life. While *Black Hawk Down* is a testament to great courage it is also a plain example of this well-meaning yet anomalous attitude to expediency in military thinking.

A US task force is sent to abduct two Somali officers in retaliation for a warlord aggression towards Americans. The targets are in a bustling Mogadishu market district where rebels mingle with townsfolk and unpredictable threats come from all angles. Bowden's writing reflects and at times caricatures the bombastic fervour of troops who believe that being US Rangers means they will dominate any encounter like a top gridiron team, the lessons of Vietnam conveniently shelved by young men eager to introduce the opposition to a world of pain. Everything starts well (except for the poor lad who misses his rope on exiting a chopper and plummets seventy feet) and prisoners are taken, but then a Black Hawk helicopter is shot down. Chillingly, if it had exploded, the mission would have been a success. The troops could have withdrawn with their prize and mourned their dead. As it is, there are survivors to evacuate and what follows is a terrifying and unforgettable backs-to-the-wall fight against overwhelming numbers.

Contemporary wars often seem as much about self-justification as they are about combat. Having such a readable, well-researched and balanced account (award winning journalist Bowden ensures that we are exposed to viewpoints from both sides) of one of the more memorable skirmishes of a recent conflict serves to make everyone's guesses about the truth behind the headlines a good deal more educated. This book also leaves you in no doubt as to the bravery – if not the unmatched skill and professionalism of which the Rangers boast – of the men involved.

Film version: *Black Hawk Down* (2001)

Read on

Road Work (NF); *Guests of the Ayatollah* (NF)

Andy McNab, *Bravo Two Zero* (NF); Jeff Struecker, *The Road to Unafraid* (NF); Damien Lewis, *Operation Certain Death* (NF)

CHESTER BROWN (b. 1960) Canada

THE PLAYBOY (1992)

There is a harmless activity that all men indulge in throughout their lives: masturbation. Because of our focus on visual stimuli nurtured by our hunting past, we men often require the erotic inspiration of the pictorial to aid our imagination in these moments of relief: pornography. It is therefore fitting that the best work of literature by far concerning these most private yet universal subjects isn't a novel or a popular science text, but a comic book.

The Sunday supplements call them 'graphic novels', getting excited about them every few years when they temporarily become legitimised as high art because someone working in mainstream literature or illustration produces an atypical one. Most men have known since they were eight that comics *are* an art form: we learned to draw figures when we were kids by copying Jack Kirby or Neal Adams and developed our taste for colourful vocabulary by reading Stan Lee's breathless prose. The underground comics of Robert Crumb and Gilbert Shelton were as much teenage meat and drink to us as those Silver Age Marvel and DC reprints.

The Playboy is a frank confessional reminiscence by writer-artist Chester Brown. With refreshing candour framed by simple yet effective drawings, Brown recounts his formative experiences as an adolescent collector of issues of ***Playboy*** magazine. Depicting himself as a tiny, hippy-haired angel flying unnoticed high above the heads of his youthful persona and suburban family, Brown unflinchingly reveals to us how he covertly bought, hid, masturbated over and guiltily destroyed the soft porn that he hints has affected his relationships with women ever since.

Showing us carnal relief, shame and the obsessive urge to hoard common to many men, Brown's boldness as an autobiographer is almost unparalleled even in the blatantly honest world of underground comics. Unlike his peers such as Dan Clowes and Harvey Pekar, Brown remains undiscovered the majority of general readers. *The Playboy* is a courageous, humane, blandly unaffected yet bittersweet work of art that all men will relate to and that every woman should read in her attempt to understand the male psyche.

Read on

I Never Liked You (chronicles more of Brown's growing pains)

Comic book angst: Peter Bagge, *Buddy Does Seattle*; Daniel Clowes, *Ghost World*; Joe Matt, *The Poor Bastard*; Harvey Pekar, *American Splendour*

CHARLES BUKOWSKI **(1920–94)** b. Germany, USA

POST OFFICE (1971)

Hank Chinaski is a misanthrope. Appalled by the soulless nature of modern man and our hideous mass production, mass media society, Chinaski escapes by drinking excessively, shacking up with wrecked yet fulsome lushes, betting on the horses and writing. But even a sot like Hank needs to pay the rent, so as Christmas approaches, our exasperated, hung-over hero takes a job at the post office.

After a few years of encountering occupational hazards like petty bosses, delivering letters during floods and coping with the unbalanced conduct of the general public, Hank hits a winning streak at the track. Sick of the arbitrary rules the post office imposes upon its employees and tired of supporting a succession of crazy, lazy women, he quits his job. Yet before too long, Chinaski is back at the old firm, taking a position as a sorting clerk that lasts for over a decade. The madness, laughter and inebriation have only just begun.

Probably the greatest novel ever written about the grinding reality of work, *Post Office* is based closely on Bukowski's own experiences, related in a deceptively simple and direct style that is easy to read, but never convincingly duplicated. Widely hailed as the definitive poet of the losers, Bukowski's funny autobiographical chronicles and eloquent free verse baldly describing his existence spent on the edge of skid row won him a huge legion of admirers. Undoubtedly the definitive men's writer of the latter half of the twentieth century, Bukowski ceased to be a cult figure tangentially associated with the dying days of the Beat Generation in the late eighties, when his works became international bestsellers. The literary equivalent of Tom Waits, Bukowski is hailed globally by critics as an authentic artist of the highest order that both the literati and everyman can effortlessly appreciate and relate to.

Read on

Ham On Rye (Chinaski's childhood); *Factotum* (Chinaski's youth); *Women, Hollywood*; *South of No North*

EDWARD BUNKER (1933–2005) USA

NO BEAST SO FIERCE (1973)

After eight years in prison, Max Dembo is determined to go straight. A formidable tearaway, Max prepares to take whatever freedom throws at him. Finding himself in his old LA stamping grounds where he plied his trade as a hood, Max feels trapped by the petty restrictions imposed upon him by his parole officer. Disillusioned by the natural unwillingness of employers to give a man with a record the opportunity of a regular job, frustrated at every turn in his attempt to walk the line of virtue, Max inevitably reconnects with the lowlife types who are the only real friends he has ever known. Max begins to thirst for vengeance and blazes with ire towards the society that has heartlessly rejected him without true hope of redemption.

As a study of animal anguish and tortured anti-heroism, ***No Beast So Fierce*** is unsurpassable. No other writer has encapsulated the career crook as the righteous enemy of our unforgiving society as effectively and passionately as Bunker, who feverishly depicts the criminal as a

Nietzschean outsider. A master of narrative polemic, Bunker increases our existential understanding of why men sometimes feel forced to choose to live beyond the law, capturing the paradox of the straight world's hypocrisy that inspires recidivism. ***No Beast So Fierce*** enrages, enthrals and overwhelms like no other crime novel and no man reads it without being changed forever.

An intermittent, habitual inmate of correctional institutions from his teens to his forties, no stranger to robbery, pimping, drug dealing and numerous other felonies, Eddie Bunker eventually made crime pay in the only way that made sense: he wrote about it. At least three of his published novels were penned while he was doing time and their blinding authenticity is immediately recognisable to the reader as little more than disguised autobiography. Bunker also advised Hollywood film-makers on how to stage heist scenes effectively (his credits for such work include ***Heat***, which features a character based on Bunker played by Jon Voigt) and wrote the screenplay of ***Runaway Train***, before belatedly finding fame through a memorable cameo as Mr Blue in *Reservoir Dogs*.

Film version: *Straight Time* (1978)

Read on

Stark; *The Animal Factory*; *Little Boy Blue*; *Dog Eat Dog*; *Mr Blue* (NF, Bunker's autobiography, which provides an interesting counterpoint to the novels that clearly draw much from his own life in crime)

READONATHEME: POLICEMAN

Good cop, bad cop, private dick: crime fiction for men

Thomas Harris, ***Red Dragon***
William Hjortsberg, ***Falling Angel***
Walter Mosley, ***Devil in a Blue Dress***
George P. Pelecanos, ***A Firing Offense***
Ian Rankin, ***Knots and Crosses***
Derek Raymond, ***I Was Dora Suarez***
Joseph Wambaugh, ***The Choirboys***
›› Colin Wilson, ***The Schoolgirl Murder Case***

JAMES LEE BURKE (b. 1936) USA

LAY DOWN MY SWORD AND SHIELD (1971)

Texas, the late 1960s. Hackberry Holland is a lawyer from a respectable Southern dynasty with a notable fondness for Jack Daniels and Mexican prostitutes. Running for congress on the Democrat ticket to satisfy his ambitious wife's desire for upward social mobility, Hack's stubborn flair for getting himself into scrapes endangers his political career when he investigates the case of Arturo Gomez, a rural labourer and union member convicted after a picket line fracas.

Examining the evidence, Hack discovers that Arturo was condemned by a kangaroo court tainted with institutional racism. When the attorney files an appeal for his Mexican friends' release and spends time drinking with the black and Hispanic Union members close to Arturo, they are victimised by redneck police. Berated by his estranged family and a hard-nosed Senator to abandon the exploited ones on the other side of the class divide and concentrate instead on his civic future, Hack elects to expiate his secret guilt over unbecoming conduct in a Korean PoW camp by standing beside the downtrodden workers no matter what the personal cost will be.

James Lee Burke is primarily known for the tough and lyrical Dave Robicheaux crime novels that started appearing in 1987. Before this Louisiana-based series made the bestseller charts, Burke produced five mainstream novels that deal with the struggle of flawed, often violent men to redeem their mistakes by finding a higher ethic within. With its civil rights focus, this is perhaps the finest of Burke's early works, displaying the moral courage and romantic tendency towards local colour that made him one of America's most celebrated contemporary writers. His skill in conveying both a man's individuality and a man's hunger – whether for sex, alcohol or justice – reveals an understanding of the male psyche found in only the most self-aware authors. Although his later books can arguably be described as formulaic despite their verbal pyrotechnics, we firmly recommend the stunning genre-blending of hardboiled crime and subtle supernatural elements to be found in Robicheaux novels ***In The Electric Mist With Confederate Dead*** and ***Burning Angel***.

See also: *100 Must-Read Crime Novels*

Read on

To The Bright and Shining Sun; *The Lost Get-Back Boogie*; *The Neon Rain* (the first Dave Robicheaux novel)

Southern discomfort: » Charles Willeford, *Miami Blues*; Jim Thompson, *The Killer Inside Me*

WILLIAM S. BURROUGHS (aka WILLIAM LEE)

(1914–97) USA

JUNKY (aka JUNKIE) (1953)

William S. Burroughs was the most notorious writer of the twentieth century. Hailing from a respectable, wealthy background, Burroughs immersed himself in the nascent counterculture of 1940s New York, where he became feted as precursor and high priest of the Beat Generation. After killing his wife in a drunken shooting accident, Burroughs relocated to Tangier, where under the influence of drugs he wrote the 'routines' that comprised his celebrated non-linear satirical masterpiece, *Naked Lunch*. Published by the notorious Olympia Press and conversely described as a groundbreaking work of genius or the contents of a sewer depending on whom you listened to, *Naked Lunch* made Burroughs internationally infamous. Over a dozen avant-garde books of varying difficulty followed, creating a cult following for the author, while many readers remained merely baffled or disgusted.

More often than not, readers approach *Naked Lunch* as their first stab at Burroughs. This is a big mistake, as the key to understanding this most challenging writer's language and recurrent obsessions lies in his first short book. Although described as a novel, ***Junky*** is thinly-masked autobiography, dealing with Burroughs' extensive experiences of heroin addiction in the decade before its publication. Written in a supremely effective, bald style, Burroughs eloquently and honestly recounts the overbearing dominion junk wields over its abusers, peppering his raptor-sharp observations with trenchant, dry wit. No other writer has ever related tales of 'Waiting For The Man' as adeptly as Burroughs, who throws in simple, evocative anecdotes of the situations and characters of Manhattan's underground scene that preceded the Beats, Warhol's Factory crowd and Bowery Punk Rock.

Despite his commercial and cult success, the unrepentant Burroughs continued to take heroin intermittently until his death. Easily the finest book ever written about drugs, the arid honesty of *Junky* is just one of many reasons why.

See also: *The Bloomsbury Good Reading Guide*; *100 Must-Read Science Fiction Novels*

Read on

Exterminator; *Port of Saints*

Ted Morgan, ***Literary Outlaw: The Life and Times of William S. Burroughs*** (NF); Will Self, ***Junk Mail*** (NF); ›› Alexander Trocchi, ***Cain's Book***

DINO BUZZATI (1906–72) Italy

THE TARTAR STEPPE (1940)

Lieutenant Giovanni Drogo leaves his hometown for a commission at a mountain fort on the edge of a vast desert that is the northern border of his country. For many years the authorities have believed that the Tartars who supposedly dwell in or beyond the wasteland might someday mount an invasion. Drogo is ready for war, but soon after he is billeted, a deadly lassitude descends upon him. Nothing is happening on the edge of the Tartar steppe. The men endlessly drill and discuss how they will defend the fort when the invaders come. Drogo applies for a transfer and a waiting game begins. Months stretch into years. Tiny figures are spotted in the remoteness of the desert: are these the Tartars or have the soldiers been deceived by mirages? Drogo's eagerness to quit his post and seek more active military duty is thwarted. He grows older and is rewarded with promotion. Then just when it feels like enemy horsemen will never be seen riding towards the fort, it seems that talk of a forthcoming battle may soon cease to be mere rumour.

Buzzati's masterpiece of a man alienated by inactivity is one of the greatest existential novels ever published, sharing the company of ***The Outsider*, *Hunger*, *Steppenwolf*** and the works of Sartre and Beckett. Despite its genius, ***The Tartar Steppe*** remains a little-known cult book deserving of great popularity. Some suggest that the story is a work of 'parallel world' SF, akin in tone to the nightmare bureaucracies of Kafka and **››** Ballard's desolate landscapes. Buzzati did indeed write some pure SF, but this was only one facet of his career, which included children's literature, short stories and other novels. A mountaineer, journalist and newspaper editor, he wrote ***The Tartar Steppe*** in 1938 while the whole of Europe, like Drogo, was waiting for war. The serene ambience of its prose, the majestic quietude of its despair and the almost comforting repose of its frustrated characters and becalmed plot sets this magnificent novel at the very peak of modernist literary achievement. If the reader has experienced the sense of being adrift that is the contingency of human existence, we cannot recommend this stunning work highly enough.

Film version: *The Desert of the Tartars* (1976)

Read on

Catastrophe

The void within: Eugene Ionesco, ***The Hermit***; Franz Kafka, ***The Castle***; Anna Kavan, ***Eagle's Nest***; Jean Paul Sartre, ***Nausea***

DEBORAH CADBURY (b. 1955) UK

SPACE RACE (2005) (NF)

While pioneering explorers bask in the glare of the spotlight, backroom boys often remain neglected. Nowhere is this dichotomy more pronounced than in the field of space exploration. In the shadow of Gagarin and Armstrong stood many technicians, but two figures are particularly notable: Werner Von Braun and Sergei Korolev.

Obsessed with astronautics, Braun joined the Nazi party to gain funding for his rocket research, building the dreaded V2s which were fired at London in the latter days of World War II. Fleeing the SS as the

Nazi regime collapsed, Braun and his team went over to the Americans and formed the technical core of NASA.

Annexing the remnants of Braun's V2 factory, the Soviets realised they needed help to catch up with their ideological enemies. Releasing rocket expert Korolev from the Siberian Gulag he was sentenced to years before after being treacherously denounced as an enemy of the party, the Russians exploited the dreams of the man they called the Chief Engineer. The triumphs of Sputnik and Vostok followed. But while Braun was a public figure in the USA, Korolev's identity remained a state secret until years after his demise.

Deborah Cadbury is a TV producer and writer whose particular talent lies in her striking aptitude for relating the gripping human stories behind key scientific endeavours. Her meticulously researched book races along, wowing the reader with its revelations like a front-rank thriller. Outlining the shameful birth of space flight in a slave labour camp, delineating the constant conflict between the driven, visionary idealism of Braun and Korolev and their Cold War paymasters' overwhelming interest in nuclear weapons, exposing the devastating truth about gantry disasters in Kazakhstan, Cadbury adroitly displays the dark side of mankind's greatest adventure. Emerging triumphantly as the figure history will laud, the Chief Engineer is unveiled as the cardinal icon of the space age – every man will find his prodigious self-sacrifice enviable, empowering and humbling.

☐ **TV series:** *Space Race* (2005)

Read on

The Dinosaur Hunters (NF); *Seven Wonders of the Industrial World* (NF)

Rocket men: Jamie Doran and Piers Bizoni, ***Starman: The Truth Behind The Legend of Yuri Gagarin*** (NF); Jim Lovell and Jeffrey Kluger, ***Apollo 13*** (NF); ›› Tom Wolfe, ***The Right Stuff*** (NF)

READONATHEME: STARMAN

Men facing the final frontier

›› J.G. Ballard, ***Memories of the Space Age***
Matthew Brzezinski, ***Red Moon Rising*** (NF)
Andrew Chaikin, ***A Man on the Moon*** (NF)
Barry N. Malzberg, ***Beyond Apollo***
Mike Mullane, ***Riding Rockets*** (NF)
Lewis Shiner, ***Frontera***
›› Dan Simmons, ***Phases of Gravity***
Andrew Smith, ***Moon Dust*** (NF)

JAMES M. CAIN (1892–1977) USA

THE POSTMAN ALWAYS RINGS TWICE (1934)

California during the Depression. Frank Chambers, an itinerant stowed away on a hay truck is thrown off his ride near a roadside diner. Bumming a meal from Nick, the Greek owner of the eatery, Frank soon finds himself accepting a job pumping gas at Nick's adjoining filling station. The drifter has a hook in him, put there by Cora, Nick's plain but shapely wife. There's just something about those lips that makes Frank want to crush them with his own.

In no time Frank and Cora are making love with animal abandon. Confessing that she has made one big mistake in her life, Cora encourages Frank to turn Nick from a cuckold into a corpse. But Cora's betrayal of Nick will drag Frank into an asphyxiating spiral of betrayal and lies that threaten to tighten around his throat like the hangman's noose. Only one of the couple will abide the ordeal to come and when the gallows is beckoning, what are the limits a man like Frank will go to save his skin?

Considered by many at the time of its publication as shockingly depraved and exploitative in its terse picturing of lust, selfishness and violence, ***The Postman Always Rings Twice*** is the epitome of the early noir novel, that sidebar of the crime genre that deals with the mentality of the amoral rather than the gentility of detection. Spare, short and unswerving in its expression of the strength of the survival instinct, this book intoxicates in its twists as the treacheries Cora and Frank pile upon each other stack up relentlessly.

A magnum opus of American existentialism, Camus himself admitted that Cain's most feted novel inspired ***The Outsider***, his own statement on masculine indifference and alienation. Despite the worship of American Noir writers by continental modernists, many readers are still to discover the brief, brusque works of Cain and his literary followers, the 'bad guy' pulp novelists who made Hammett and Chandler look effete. Over seventy years on, Cain's dizzying story remains as compulsive and significant as ever.

Film versions: *The Postman Always Rings Twice* (1946) and (1981)

See also: *100 Must-Read Crime Novels*

Read on

Double Indemnity; *Mildred Pierce*

Femme fatales: Lawrence Block, *The Girl with the Long Green Heart*; Delacorta, *Diva*; James Ellroy, *The Black Dahlia*; David Goodis, *The Blonde on the Street Corner*

CARLOS CASTANEDA (1931–98) Brazil

THE TEACHINGS OF DON JUAN (1968) (NF)

Ever wanted to leap tall buildings in a single bound or be a dog for a day? The Yaqui Indian medicine man Don Juan can show you how to perform these and other superhuman feats claims Carlos Castaneda in the first of his disquisitions on a particularly potent brand of Native American wisdom. Key to success is the foul-tasting peyote plant that introduces the open-minded initiate to worlds within worlds; places where laws of physics and the very fabric of reality are torn apart and reconstructed.

Before he can be privy to any arcane secrets, Castaneda must display self-knowledge by passing an abstract test. Then he gets to chew on some peyote. This is drug taking as ritual; a vice invested with the respectability of religion. The visions and outlandish experiences which befall the young anthropology student are highly evocative and can be read as fascinating, psychedelic dreams or spiritual awakening. Either way, *The Teachings of Don Juan* is an incisive account of man's obsession with gurus, written by a serious minded, intelligent individual who is clearly no mug. Castaneda's apprenticeship is long and involves both mundane and esoteric tasks, many of them painful. At times he is sorely tempted to quit but the promised rewards are alluring and his curiosity must be assuaged. There are dark forces out there though – enemies as well as allies and he must be ever watchful.

Although there is arguably no concrete evidence to suggest that belief really can move mountains, powerful convictions sometimes make faith seem real and who is to say that Don Juan's other dimensions have not been *made* real by the concerted belief of generations of Native Americans. They are concrete enough for those who follow the way of Mescalito (as peyote is also known) and Castaneda is convinced, although others have raised serious questions as to the validity of his books. At least two studies have concluded that his writings are fiction, but that his ideas and philosophies hold water nevertheless. More pertinently, his work is about man seeking guidance outside conventional religion, a craving which is almost as prevalent today as it was in the sixties.

See also: *100 Must-Read Life-Changing Books*

Sequels: (all NF) *A Separate Reality*; *Journey to Ixtlan*; *Tales of Power*; *The Second Ring of Power*; *The Eagle's Gift*; *The Fire From Within*; *The Power of Silence*; *The Art of Dreaming*; *The Wheel of Time*

Read on

Paulo Coelho, *The Pilgrimage* (NF); Frederick Lenz, *Surfing the Himalayas*; Dan Millman, *The Way of the Peaceful Warrior* (NF); James Redfield, *The Celestine Prophecy*

WALTER VAN TILBURG CLARK (1909–71) USA

THE OX-BOW INCIDENT (1940)

Early springtime in the West: cowboys Art Croft and Gil Carter ride into Bridger's Wells, a small town that is home to a number of cattle drovers. After months on the range, suffering from mild cabin fever, the partners head for the saloon. Some whiskey, some poker and a fight naturally follow before a youngster bursts in to report that another local cowboy has been shot dead by rustlers. The Sheriff is out of town, everyone's blood is up and shortly a posse begins to coalesce. While the majority hunger for swift retribution, some argue that without proper restraint what some men describe as justice will merely be lawless vigilante vengeance. As night descends upon Bridger's Wells is seems likely the posse will become a lynching party. Soon Croft will discover that the bone-freezing chill of the western night is nothing beside the coldness that lies within men's hearts.

Classic Western novels are surprising to generations raised on the amorality of spaghetti western movies, for they often contain as much philosophising as action, debating suitable ethical codes for a new frontier where the right to bear arms was a necessity. Although Wister's *The Virginian* (1902) elevated the Western from its pulp origins to the status of a craft, *The Ox-Bow Incident* is generally regarded as the first work of literature to emerge from the genre. A tense narrative containing all the archetypal elements readers expect from a Western, the book describes the close camaraderie arising from partnerships tested in the great outdoors while questioning the negative aspects of male bonding. Clark challenges the reader with serious arguments about the individual's ability to exhibit the courage necessary to stand aside from the cowardice of mob rule. *The Ox-Bow Incident* is effective as art and entertainment, suggesting that a man doesn't always have to do what a man has to do.

A University lecturer and poet, Clark was only active as a novelist for ten years. While many famous Western novels now seem staid, Clark's masterwork still provides the white-knuckle suspense and moral commitment contemporary readers would expect of the genre.

Film version: *The Ox-Bow Incident* (1943)

Read on

Western alternatives: » James Lee Burke, *Two For Texas*; Zane Grey, *Riders of the Purple Sage*; Oakley Hall, *Warlock*; » Cormac McCarthy, *Blood Meridian*; Wallace Stegner, *Angle of Repose*

JEREMY CLARKSON (b. 1960) UK

I KNOW YOU GOT SOUL (2005) (NF)

I Know You Got Soul is a gloriously subjective list of engineering triumphs that the author considers to be more than mere machines, their special qualities arising as much from their flaws as from any innate handsomeness or efficiency. Welcoming us into his very masculine domain, Clarkson offers enthusiasm, humorous asides and justification for the preference of many men for exotic transport over – say – female company. These chosen few are tenderly eulogised whilst the opposition is cruelly defamed.

So – cars: drive a Rolls Royce and everyone hates you, kidding themselves that something other than pure envy has invoked their ire. Fictional spaceships? Clarkson's geeky comparison between the ***USS Enterprise*** and the ***Millennium Falcon*** will engage you while confirming that yes, you *are* a total saddo.

Clarkson's prose style is the same as that which spouts from his straight-talking gob on ***Top Gear***, and it is therefore to his credit as a vocal expounder of lad philosophy that the book flows along so naturally. The French are Johnny Frog, Russians are called Ivan and Concorde was worth any amount of taxpayers cash even if all most of us could ever do was gawp at it from 60,000 feet away.

As well as his comic skill (his retelling of the dogged persistence of von Zeppelin producing a series of useless airships is classic Monty Python), Clarkson has a gift for expressing scale, whether it be the stupendous size of a jumbo jet or the hideous loss of life in a maritime disaster – a most striking chapter deals with the ***SS Great Britain*** and respectfully enumerates the human cost of ocean liners sunk in the Atlantic, where the general principle of evacuation was crew first and sod the passengers.

Clarkson's job is to speak for the repressed bloke within us and although he has been associated with the odd unreconstructed opinion, fragments of what he says in the jewel in BBC2's ratings crown and writes in ***The Sunday Times*** will strike a chord even with the newest of new men, though they will of course deny this (especially to their wives).

Read on

The World According to Clarkson (NF); *Clarkson on Cars* (NF)

James May, ***Notes from the Hard Shoulder*** (NF); Perry McCarthy, ***Flat Out, Flat Broke*** (NF); Diana Preston, ***Wilful Murder: The Sinking of the Lusitania*** (NF)

JONATHAN COE (b. 1961) UK

THE ROTTER'S CLUB (2001)

The early seventies: wild musical experimentation and polar politics, angry socialists banging heads with complacent traditionalists, confused boys searching for an informed pathway to adulthood. In a posh Birmingham school with a solitary black pupil nicknamed Rastus, Ben Trotter (Bent Rotter) finds religion when God delivers a pair of trunks to him just as he resigns himself to the humiliation of a nude swimming lesson. His sister's boyfriend Malcolm is killed in an IRA pub bombing, but the latter's passion for avant garde music lives on in Ben. Inopportunely, punk arrives to quash Ben's prog rock ambitions.

On the other side of the social divide is Bill Anderton, union man at the factory where Ben's dad is a manager. Bill is keen to uphold the moral rights of his fellow workers, whilst countering an insidious, nationwide racism. Bill's affair with a secretary ends abruptly when she vanishes, her sister Claire later coming to him seeking clues. Bill's son Doug is a school-friend of Ben, and one of the few to challenge the hand-me-down, pro-establishment views of his middle class peers. Doug's relationship with Claire is one of the countless connecting threads in a complex but ultimately satisfying tale.

In the achingly hilarious world of Bent Rotter, the written word is a constant threat to the status quo (watch out for the priceless 'letters to the editor' from a non-existent parent). Ben's magazine article criticising his idol's lacklustre portrayal of Desdemona to Rastus's Othello in the school play has an unexpected effect as does an overblown love letter sent by a teacher to Philip's mum. Throughout the book, liaisons are formed and broken, and various key themes swim ingeniously in and out of focus.

The Rotter's Club is a classic of political satire by a writer whose left-facing allegiance is unambiguous, but who possesses the rare talent of creating plausible, complex characters to represent alternate view-points. Coe can do comic and sad with equal facility, and his novels are always a treat. He, like Ben and Doug, went to an exclusive Midlands school.

TV series: *The Rotter's Club* (2005)
Sequel: *The Closed Circle*
Read on
What a Carve Up!; *The House of Sleep*
Hanif Kuerishi, ***The Buddha of Suburbia***; Tim Lott, ***Rumours of a Hurricane***

DOUGLAS COUPLAND (b. 1961) Canada

GENERATION X (1991)

Andy and his friends Dag and Claire live in a world drained of its vitality by previous generations; a place grown impersonal and just too darned big, where negatives swamp any pin-prick of optimism there is to be found. Vapid slogans rule, depressing new buzzwords abound and the dispossessed young things resort to telling each other stories in order both to lampoon and escape their stultifying existence. Pouring scorn on the vacant posturing of yuppies (an especially memorable episode involves Claire's boyfriend drizzling roses onto her as she sleeps, only for her to discover that he buys them dirt cheap from a roadside vendor) and the new age pretensions of relatives, these twenty-somethings scavenge for meaning, trawlling their memories for moments which might act as some kind of redemptive medicine.

The original *Generation X* was a book published in the 1960s about Mods and Rockers. While some would argue that Coupland's borrowing of the title reveals the paucity and world-weariness of the slacker imagination, we would suggest that the author endowed the term with greater relevance, grouping together an all but invisible, intelligent underclass, passively protesting by opting out of the rat race. *Generation X* differs from your average tale about the activities of slackers because it is not slackly written: Coupland's observation of sharp-witted McJob workers displays genius.

This was Coupland's first novel, and subsequent books have cemented his reputation as a character analyst whilst taking on subjects such as the IT business and religion, often with a subtly supernatural slant. His experimentation with structure is evident in his forays into Pop Art, and he has also written for the stage.

Read on

Hey Nostradamus!; *JPod*

» Bret Easton Ellis, *Less Than Zero*; » Chuck Palanhiuk, *Survivor*; Jack Handey, *Deep Thoughts*

JAMES CRUMLEY (b. 1939) USA

ONE TO COUNT CADENCE (1969)

Despite a degree that brands him as an intellectual, Sergeant Jacob 'Slag' Krummell is descended from a long line of warriors, feeling the lure of Valhalla in his veins. Taking a posting in the Philippines as American Military Advisors unofficially begin to appear in Vietnam, Krummell finds himself commanding a ragbag group of whoring, drunken soldiers. Immediately at home with this irreverent khaki crew, the sergeant settles into a raucous routine of goldbricking with his new buddies. Pre-eminent amongst these is Joe Morning, a natural rebel with a bookshelf full of Dostoevsky and Sartre.

Although Morning's problems with authority are not unique, his outrageous approach makes him a foil to the viscerally intelligent Krummell. The latter rejects Morning's liberal standpoint as naive, while his own belief in the historical nobility of killing is bolstered by his bellicosity as a brawler, boozer and womaniser. But when Krummell's undisciplined cadre are flown to Vietnam, the Sergeant finds time to repent of his nihilism when he and his beloved comrades are plunged into the inferno of the war America could not win.

Poetic in its style, thoughtful in its meditations and urgently earthy in its depictions of military male bonding, ***One To Count Cadence*** is packed with superb character studies, beautifully evoked tropical imagery and more than a smattering of literary self-consciousness. Reminiscent of films like ***Platoon*** and ***Full Metal Jacket*** in its perceptive study of men and their philosophies in situations of extreme stress, lauded by many of the veterans who have read it, this book may well be the great forgotten Vietnam novel despite the fact that only a small amount of its action takes place there.

James Crumley served three years in the US Army, taught at several universities and made his name with the celebrated Chandler-on-cocaine crime novels that followed ***One To Count Cadence***, his first book.

See also: *100 Must-Read Crime Novels*

Read on

The Last Good Kiss; *The Wrong Case*

The Nam: Gustav Hasford, ***The Short Timers*** (aka ***Full Metal Jacket***); Michael Herr, ***Dispatches*** (NF); Robert Mason, ***Chickenhawk*** (NF); Bao Nihn, ***The Sorrow of War***

MILES DAVIS (1926–91) USA

MILES: THE AUTOBIOGRAPHY (1989) (NF) (with Quincy Troupe)

Jazz trumpeter Miles Davis was the epitome of cool. Period. For over thirty years he was recognised as one of the vital pioneers of new music per se, pioneering not only fresh directions in jazz, but exercising influence over fields like rock, funk and ambient music. What separated Miles from many of his peers was not just his chops as an instrumentalist or his inventiveness as a composer, but his facility in judging which musicians would be the most innovative to play and write with. While other jazz masters would grandstand, dominating their combos, Miles knew when not to blow, when to let other composer's talents expand unchained. A hard taskmaster famous for his quietness and taciturnity, Miles always commanded the willing respect and love of several generations of musicians.

Growing up on the right side of the tracks (he was the son of a middle-class dentist), Miles moved to Manhattan to study music at the prestigious Julliard college. His hidden intention was to get a real education in the clubs, sitting in with revolutionary beboppers like Charlie Parker. Before too long, Miles was cutting 78s, cultivating a heroin habit, pimping street girls and playing a significant part in the birth of modern jazz. Seasoned throughout with casual jive-talking obscenities and seething indictments of white man's racism, Miles' fierce energy ripples through a litany of anecdotes featuring all the important personalities in the pantheon of modern jazz – for music buffs, this book is simply orgasmic in its revelations.

Admired equally by the literati, film stars, hip kids, beatniks and nodding gone cats with photographic recall of matrix numbers and recording date lineups, Miles Davis was one of black culture's first megastars. Although this undeniably egocentric autobiography is rarely humble, Davis' integrity as an artist is not compromised by the brutally honest tone in which he confesses his many failings and indulgences. Even when describing his addictive personality and jealousy of his wives (things he is clearly not proud of), Miles does not flinch from the facts. A scorching exposition of success and shortcoming, ***Miles*** confirms that most other music memoirs are merely polite fluff.

Read on

Richard Cook and Brian Morton, ***The Penguin Guide to Jazz on CD*** (NF – a reference book that is also a beautifully written meditation on the music); Geoff Dwyer, ***But Beautiful***; Mezz Mezrow and Bernard Wolfe, ***Really The Blues*** (NF); Charles Mingus, ***Beneath The Underdog*** (NF); Michael Ondaatje, ***Coming Through Slaughter***

LEN DEIGHTON (b. 1929) UK

THE IPCRESS FILE (1962)

London at the height of the Cold War: our sardonic narrator is transferred from Military Intelligence to a secret service unit based in seedy Fitzrovia. His new boss is Dalby, a spy investigating the disappearances of several top biochemists. Thwarted in his mission to recover the latest hostage from his kidnappers, our hero takes a plane to Beirut, where he and Dalby set up an explosive night-time ambush in the Lebanese countryside to retrieve the scientist. Upon travelling to an American air base on a Pacific atoll where a neutron bomb is due to be tested, the neophyte spy is dragged swiftly into a deadly, multi-facetted web of deceit and confusion. In the sphere of espionage, trust and certainty are meaningless concepts.

Although many have thrilled to the film ***The Ipcress File***, the movie is thin, simplistic stuff compared to the novel: it has a wider canvas (the film never leaves London) and its story and characters are more impenetrable. Despite Michael Caine's suitably insolent performance, he is not the Harry Palmer of the book – in fact, our spy is nameless, doesn't wear glasses and doesn't practise gourmet cooking. Instead, he's a history enthusiast bothered by the implications of his expense account, whose actions throughout the novel sometimes seem as suspect as those of his quarries. The famously labyrinthine plot is acutely challenging but considerably rewarding, furnishing the reader with a plausible insight into how paranoid and circumspect the world of the real spy must be.

Originally trained as an artist, Len Deighton transformed the espionage genre with his first novel. The focus on shabby offices, mundane paperwork, enigmatic dialogue and backstabbing double-crosses (held together by opaque motivations and the ambiguities of compartmentalised intelligence) made James Bond look like a spoilt dilettante. The figure many call Harry Palmer remains an icon of spy fiction, being easy to identify with due to his occasional vulnerability, bold impudence and casual toughness. Every man should read ***The Ipcress File***, its clipped language and realistic detail representing the highest watermark the thriller genre has reached to date.

Film version: *The Ipcress File* (1965)
Sequels: *Horse Under Water*; *Funeral in Berlin*; *Billion Dollar Brain*; *Spy Story*

Read on

Eric Ambler, *The Mask of Dimitrios*; Frederick Forsyth, *The Day of the Jackal*; Robert Harris and Jeremy Paxman, *A Higher Form of Killing: The Secret History of Gas and Germ Warfare* (NF)

ISABELLE EBERHARDT (1877–1904) Switzerland

THE OBLIVION SEEKERS (translated 1972)

If there is one thing men value socially more than the company of other males, it is the friendship of a woman able to hold her own as an honorary 'one of the boys'. We admire the confidence, try-anything-once attitude and good-natured commitment to participation such women exhibit. Sometimes we are even lucky enough to marry them.

Today, we might claim that Isabelle Eberhardt might have been happy to match us pint for pint. The illegitimate offspring of parents who boasted of Russian, Armenian and German ancestry, Eberhardt was brought up by her former Orthodox priest father, who made her wear boy's clothes and perform manual labour alongside her brothers. When her mother died, the inconsolable girl wailed that she wanted to die. Her father's response was to offer her a pistol so that she could commit suicide. A full-blown nihilist, daddy instilled in his daughter a healthy disregard for conventional ideas and respectable notions of morality.

In adulthood Eberhardt relocated to French North Africa. Still wearing male garb, she was accepted by the locals while scandalising European expatriates. She smoked dope, drank booze and practised free love. Converting to Sufism despite her mother's Jewish background, Eberhardt found tolerance and wisdom in this branch of Islam. But did she find peace within herself?

The Oblivion Seekers contains intoxicating stories, essays and other vignettes that reveal a woman who was most fulfilled when she lost herself in remoteness. Full of serene, hawk-like observations of desert life and stern meditations on the nature of freedom, her bracingly arid prose is unsentimental in character yet surprisingly robust in its tenderness. Hailed as the Godmother of the counterculture, comparable in her best moments to the great twentieth century modernist writers, Eberhardt was a fascinating pioneer of both alternative living and impressionistic writing. Her writings are required reading for all freethinkers, making men feel unadventurous while awakening women to their potential as individuals. Translated by the brilliant novelist Paul Bowles, *The Oblivion Seekers* should sit on your bookshelf alongside the works of Burroughs and Camus.

Read on

Prisoner of Dunes (NF); *In The Shadow of Islam* (NF)
Paul Bowles, *The Sheltering Sky*; Anna Kavan, *Ice*; Lee Ranaldo, *Road Movies* (NF)

READONATHEME: WOMAN

Grinding out the gender/genre division: books by women men can enjoy

Jane Bowles, *Two Serious Ladies*
Angela Carter, *The Passion of New Eve*
Marianne Faithfull, *Memories Dreams Reflections* (NF)
›› Patricia Highsmith, *Found in the Street*
Tove Jansson, *The Winter Book*
Anna Kavan, *My Madness: The Selected Writings*
Ursula K. Le Guin, *The Left Hand of Darkness*
Anais Nin, *The Spy in the House of Love*
Valerie Solanas, *The SCUM Manifesto* (NF)
Muriel Spark, *The Drivers' Seat*

BRET EASTON ELLIS (b. 1964) USA

AMERICAN PSYCHO (1991)

Sex, cocaine, designer garb and lightweight pop are the diet of body beautiful yuppie serial killer Patrick Bateman. The eighties Wall Street greed of ›› Tom Wolfe's *Bonfire of the Vanities* is here in spades, as is the hollow sound of countless brand names being dropped. In Bateman's circle, the priorities are your hairline, abdominals and bank account. These men admit to only two types of people: the mega-rich (men with the costliest and coolest boy toys – women with perfect hardbodies) and the layabout poor. They eat what and where trendy guides tell them to, irrespective of personal taste, and their uniform habits mean that cases of mistaken identity are commonplace, a fact that affable maniac Bateman uses to his advantage.

You know the violence is coming and the wait makes it that more intense. When pandemonium is unleashed, emerging from the morass of shallow chat and complacent glitz, it strikes like a freeway pile-up. Having ignored or mocked beggars day after day, Bateman whimsically and gruesomely blinds one, before strolling off to celebrate the casual atrocity. Graphic sex fuses consummately with blatant violence, blurring the boundary between procreation and mayhem. The frequency, brutality and creativity of Bateman's murders escalates to a truly sickening level, but our perpetrator remains emotionally numb – the psychosis governs him but it neither troubles nor thrills him.

Although at first glance it appears to be nothing but an attempt to shock, *American Psycho* is actually an astonishing consumerist tragi-comedy with a narrative trick in its tail that possibly influenced » Chuck Palahniuk's *Fight Club*. Ellis himself won't read *American Psycho*, as he is disturbed and haunted by his 'villain' – an affliction explored in the partly autobiographical horror novel *Lunar Park*. Young wasters, party people and the dispossessed populate Ellis's books and he became known as one of the literary Brat Pack of authors who found early success alongside the likes of Jay McInerney.

Read on

Glamorama

» Jim Carroll, *The Basketball Diaries* (NF); Douglas Coupland, *Hey*

Nostradamus!; Don Delillo, ***Americana***; Toby Young, ***How To Lose Friends and Alienate People*** (NF)

MICK FARREN (b. 1943) UK

THE TALE OF WILLY'S RATS (1974)

Lou Francis is lead singer of Willy's Rats, a group with the attitude of The Stones, whose songs drip the blues-based heaviness of Zeppelin while projecting a decadent sexuality that rivals that of The Velvet Underground. Indulging in the excesses of dope, wallowing in the wicked joys of abusing masochistic groupies, waited on hand and foot by roadies, the Rats never fail to deliver a gorgeous noise crammed with mojo and angst. But despite their chart and critical success, Lou is intermittently worried by anonymous threats of onstage assassination during an upcoming US tour.

Beginning with Lou's serendiptous discovery of Elvis in the fifties and moving through his rock and roll apprenticeship via a Shadows-type combo, the folk movement, the blues boom, the birth of hippy counter-culture and the full-blown psychedelia of swinging London circa 1967, ***The Tale of Willy's Rats*** is a tightrope journey through the history of British rock that makes the reader feel like he was there. Feedback from epochal gigs at Hyde Park, the apocalypse of Altamont, the casual misogyny of big tour entourages and the acid tests of the UFO club echoes throughout the pages of this extraordinary novel.

As most readers who love music know, novels about rock are almost uniformly appalling and embarrassing, no matter how good the writer.

Leaving behind literary prizewinners and celebrated best-selling novelists who can only choke in his dust, the former *NME* journalist and ex-boyfriend of Germaine Greer produced the only rock novel that is essential reading. Capturing those sublime moments of amplified ecstasy convincingly in fiction is no mean feat and only Mick Farren has truly accomplished it. Formerly an Afro-toting, leather jacketed, agit-propagandist and alternative rock star himself (fronting sonic terrorists The Deviants and writing lyrics for their speedfreak successors The Pink Fairies), Farren was one of the visionary hooligans who predicted punk. Today he resides in New York, writing science fiction novels and trying to stay out of trouble.

Read on

Give the Anarchist a Cigarette (autobiography); *The Black Leather Jacket* (NF)

Rock fantasies: Brian Aldiss, *Brothers of the Head*; Todd Haynes, *Velvet Goldmine* (Screenplay); George R.R. Martin, *The Armageddon Rag*

IAN FLEMING (1908–64) UK

YOU ONLY LIVE TWICE (1964)

Traumatised by the murder of his bride by SPECTRE, James Bond has lapsed into apathy. Summoned to M's office, 007 is ready to tender his resignation when his superior tells him he is being assigned a new mission in the Land of the Rising Sun.

In Japan, Bond contacts Tiger Tanaka, head of the Nipponese secret service after being initiated into local society by bullish Antipodean agent Dikko Henderson. Bond is meant to obtain details of CIA code-cracking computers from Tanaka, but the formidable oriental needs a favour. On a small island off the mainland, a European botanist known as Dr Shatterhand has purchased a castle whose verdant gardens have been cultivated with poisonous plants, snakes and arachnids. Given the Japanese penchant for suicide as a nepenthe for dishonour, people keep disappearing into the environs of this lethal enclave, embarrassing the authorities. Receiving Ninja training, Bond agrees to aid Tanaka in investigating the problem, but nothing can prepare him for the revelations that await him within the walls of the 'Castle of Death'.

The recent cinematic reinvention of Bond was largely successful due to the scriptwriters' fealty to the demeanour and spirit of the master spy as he is in the original novels. The Bond stories are not dated, but of their time, remaining relevant for a contemporary audience, containing all the grit, despair, sadism, sex and treachery present in the film ***Casino Royale*** (2006). You might have seen the movies, but the real Bond can only be truly appreciated by those who have read the books.

The last but one of the series, ***You Only Live Twice*** is probably the most ornate and imaginative Bond story and certainly one of the most world-weary, making it an ideal introduction for those wishing to compare the original 007 with the earlier film incarnations, which had become cheesy even before Sean Connery quit. The exotic locales and fantastic plot clash intoxicatingly with Fleming's pronounced streak of ruthless conservatism, while the ebullience of his characters ensures they are much more than wooden ciphers. While his works are first rate escapism rather than art, Fleming's worldliness and personal experience of international intrigue set him above his imitators, with over sixty million sales confirming his status as the grandmaster of the glamorous espionage thriller.

Film version: *You Only Live Twice* (1967)
Sequel: *The Man With the Golden Gun*
Read on
Stephen Dorrill, ***MI6*** (NF); Sebastian Faulks, ***Devil May Care***; **››** Graham Greene and Sir Hugh Greene, ***The Spies' Bedside Book*** (classic anthology of fiction and non-fiction); Ben Macintyre, ***Agent Zigzag*** (NF)

GEORGE MACDONALD FRASER

(1926–2008) UK

FLASHMAN (1969)

It's not easy to feel kinship with a rapist, especially one who jovially admits that he would have repeated the crime were it not that every other woman he fancied was either already willing or susceptible to other forms of coercion. Perhaps his being at a historical remove from contemporary man – as well as the comic tone of his adventures – is what warms us to Harry Flashman (the school bully who first appeared in Thomas Hughes's *Tom Brown's Schooldays*) as he swaggers and copulates his way through some of the most memorable conflicts in the history of the British Empire.

Flashman's dubious morality is clear from the moment he protests that expulsion from school will break his mother's heart – despite the fact that she is long dead. But while his memoirs are honest in their admission of instances of cowardice, Flashman generally treats life as nothing more than a great game. Indeed, on the occasion of almost dying in the service of the 11th Light Dragoons in Afghanistan, he compares the experience to being crushed in a rugby scrum.

Early in his military career, Flashman cheats his way out of a duel, gaining unwarranted repute as a marksman in the process and this, combined with an alacrity in learning languages (largely during bedtime trysts with female servants overseas) leads to special assignments and ever greater renown through the course of eleven sequels. Appealing to the inner bounder in many of us, Flashman's knockabout exploits have won him a legion of fans.

Fraser fought in Burma during World War II. He presents the Flashman sequence as a memoir he has merely edited, a common device employed in Victorian adventure novels. His extensive research and first hand experience of the locations featured in the books have rendered them accurate enough for some to have fallen for the tongue-in-cheek claim that they are true stories. Fraser spent some time working as a journalist and contributed to screenplays for *The Three Musketeers* (1973) and *Octopussy* (1983).

Film version: *Royal Flash* (1975)
Sequels: *Royal Flash*; *Flash for Freedom!*; *Flashman at the Charge*; *Flashman in the Great Game*; *Flashman's Lady*; *Flashman and the Redskins*; *Flashman and the Dragon*; *Flashman and the Mountain of Light*; *Flashman and the Angel of the Lord*; *Flashman and the Tiger*; *Flashman on the March*

Read on

Quartered Safe Out Here (NF)

Peter Hopkirk, *The Great Game* (NF); Rudyard Kipling, *The Man Who Would Be King & Other Stories*; Joe Roberts, *Three Quarters of a Footprint* (NF)

ALASDAIR GRAY (b. 1934) UK

1982 JANINE (1984)

Jock is a security installations supervisor, travelling around his native Scotland checking on the alarms his company maintains for business clients. Middle-aged, divorced, conservative, often inebriated, he spends most evenings in anonymous hotel rooms. Lying in lonely beds he fantasies about women. His mind runs through idealised sexual scenarios of a mildly fetishistic character – Jock's imaginary female consorts wear white silk blouses, satin brassieres, particular types of jeans, skirts and shoes. As Jock is a devotee of bondage, his dreamgirls are often tied up. Although these erotic musings help him pass the time before whiskey brings oblivion, Jock also reflects upon his past as a young student in Glasgow. Recruited by a theatre group as their electrician and lighting engineer, Jock's practical, scientific demeanour undergoes an internal transformation as he awakens to the aesthetic importance of his role. When the group take their play to the Edinburgh Fringe while Cook, Moore, Bennet and Miller are the toast of the main festival, Jock's finds himself at a turning point that will determine his future happiness.

Alasdair Gray is the most gifted Scots writer since ›› Alexander Trocchi. Encompassing both classic and modern literary techniques, Gray additionally uses his skill as an illustrator to punctuate his books, incorporating drawings and unusual typographical experiments. Every element of a Gray book is usually part of the story he is telling, even the blurbs and designs on the jacket. Although his substantial literary fantasy ***Lanark*** won him the most critical acclaim, it is the vastly underrated ***1982 Janine*** that will immediately resonate with male readers. Very much a book of two halves, the repetitive litany of Jock's interior sexual fantasies will remind men of their own erotic obsessions while the tale of Jock's theatrical experiences and their quietly tragic fallout makes the reader reflect on the wisdom of the choices made in his own life.

Read on

Something Leather

Scots man: Iain Banks, ***The Wasp Factory***; Andrew Greig, ***Electric Brae***; Neil M. Gunn, ***Blood Hunt***; James Kellman, ***You Have To Be Careful In The Land of the Free***

GRAHAM GREENE (1904–91) UK

THE MINISTRY OF FEAR (1943)

On the advice of a medium, Arthur Rowe wins a cake at a country fair by guessing its weight. Immediately he attracts the attentions of certain parties who are determined to retrieve the cake for some unknown reason. Such are Rowe's romantic inclinations that he actively seeks to embroil himself in the strangeness of the situation, hiring a private detective and tracking down the medium. Attending a séance at which a man dies, Rowe finds himself the prime suspect. On the run, he falls in with Anna, whose mysterious brother's activities are shrouded in secrecy.

After Rowe suffers sudden amnesia, Anna's reappearance drives him to forsake blissful ignorance and continue his quest for the truth, the backdrop of nightly Blitz bombings adding a terrifying extra dimension to this dramatic mystery. Rowe's wish for an exhilarating life is common in men harnessed to the workaday world, but the question is how much excitement can one man deal with?

Graham Greene classed ***The Ministry of Fear*** as an entertainment, yet it is superbly written and touches upon issues he took very seriously – dreams, loneliness and suicide. A master of disguise, Greene created so many false impressions of his character that no casual acquaintance could claim to know him. What is certain is that he was a real man's man: an amiable scoundrel, a lover of women and alcohol, described by V.S. Pritchett as genially subversive.

Like the author himself, many of Greene's most powerful characters are Catholics whose faith causes them ethical conundrums. There is the youthful gangster of ***Brighton Rock***, the alcoholic priest of ***The Power and the Glory*** and the unfaithful husband of ***The Heart of the Matter***. However, its fair to say he could have chosen any other doctrinal peg on which to hang his protagonists' insecurities, once writing that once a Catholic could not help having sympathy for any faith that was sincerely held. Long regarded as a world class writer, Greene was never too precious to let art get in the way of creating superlative recreational reading matter.

Film version: *The Ministry of Fear* (1944)

Read on

The Human Factor; *Brighton Rock*; *The Heart of the Matter*
Joseph Conrad, *The Secret Agent*; Stanislav Lem, *The Investigation*

STEPHEN GREGORY (b. 1952) UK

THE CORMORANT (1986)

When the unnamed narrator and his wife inherit a cottage in North Wales, they gratefully escape the drudgery of their teaching jobs in Derbyshire. Their benefactor is the narrator's uncle and there is one condition in the will: the couple will keep the house only if they look after the formers' pet cormorant, which he rescued from an oil spill when the bird was a juvenile.

The couple and their toddling son settle into their new home, bank balance bulging from the sale of their old house, the narrator setting to work on writing a textbook. All is idyllic until the cormorant is delivered. The bird is a sheeny black demon, bursting from its crate, excreting everywhere, pecking at its new owners with a razor-sharp bill. Confined to a cage in the back yard, loathed by the lady of the house, the bird starts to exert a strange fascination for the narrator. Taking the bird fishing, he is gradually won over by the cormorant's effortless hunting accomplishments, but his wife is troubled by the infernal malevolence the unwelcome member of the ménage exhibits. The cormorant seems to be more than just an animal: is the narrator deluded, or is the taciturn influence of his uncle embodied by the creature's threatening, unpredictable behaviour?

At 148 pages ***The Cormorant*** is a small masterpiece, the first novel by a very talented writer who has just broken a long silence with his new book *The Perils and Dangers of this Night*. Warning man of the dangers of anthropomorphism, Gregory limpidly conveys the motiveless malignance of the cormorant without ever descending into purple prose. His quietly plangent descriptions of the chill greyness of the Welsh coast are the envy of many nature writers while his confidence in presenting the value of family life will resound with husbands and fathers. Falling somewhere between early Iain Banks and **››** M. John Harrison in its approach, the book also contains the grains of a ghost story. A tragic tale with flashes of horror, ***The Cormorant*** incisively suggests that in our confrontations with wildlife, perhaps we too become victims of our own cruelty.

TV play: *The Cormorant* (1993)

Read on

The Woodwitch; ***The Blood of Angels***

J.A. Baker, ***The Peregrine*** (NF); Barry Hines, ***Kes***; Gavin Maxwell, ***Ring of Bright Water*** (NF)

ERNESTO 'CHE' GUEVARA (1928–67) Argentina

THE MOTORCYCLE DIARIES (1993) (NF)

In 1951 Ernesto Guevara and his friend Alberto Granado set off by motorcycle on a trip around South America. Ernesto's diary of events formed the basis of a book that was published much later when what might have seemed a youthful folly at the time had crystallized into the formative year of a man who, along with Castro, became synonymous with Communist rebellion.

Ernesto is a romantic young philosopher studying medicine. Alberto, several years his senior, hungers for heroic adventure. Their journey begins inauspiciously with illness and multiple crashes as they bully their Norton 500 across yielding sands but such misfortunes are countered by the generosity of strangers and the allure of pretty girls, and at times they progress with sated appetites. The vagaries of fortune result in Ernesto shooting their host's dog (believing it to be a puma), being feted as a leprosy expert and defecating over a German family's peaches. There is much running away. There is also a frustrated anguish at social injustice, and Guevara harbours dreams of alleviating the plight of the poor worldwide. In fact, he seems to mature very suddenly, focusing on political concerns for long periods of the book before reverting to the mischievous scamp again later on.

Of course, visiting interesting places and commenting upon them does not make you an interesting person, but Che was exceptional. ***The Motorcycle Diaries*** may have inspired young men everywhere to speed off into the unknown (although Guevara's bike actually conks out quite early in the piece) but more importantly, they bring context to the revolutionary escapades of his later life. They are a valuable document in the history of a key figure of political insurgency and evidence of an ordinary young man, not always true to the principles for which we remember him – but then, how annoying would he be if he were?

Film version: *The Motorcycle Diaries* (2004)

Read on

Bolivian Diary (NF); *Guerilla Warfare* (NF)

John Lee Anderson, ***Che Guevara: A Revolutionary Life*** (NF); Ewan McGregor and Charley Boorman, ***Long Way Round*** (NF); Robert Pirsig, ***Zen and the Art of Motorcycle Maintenance***

READ ON A THEME: WISE MAN

Bright chaps, big ideas: popular science and zeitgeist philosophy (all NF)

John Berger, *Ways of Seeing*
Richard Dawkins, *The God Delusion*
John Gray, *Straw Dogs*
Stephen Hawking, *A Brief History of Time*
Werner Heisenberg, *Physics and Philosophy*
Roger Lewin, *Bones of Contention*
James Miller, *The Passion of Michel Foucault*
Ray Monk, *Wittgenstein: The Duty of Genius*
Francis Wheen, *How Mumbo Jumbo Conquered the World*
Michael White, *A Teaspoon and an Open Mind*

BEN HAMPER (b. 1955) USA

RIVETHEAD (1991) (NF)

How much do you know about yourself if you've never worked a night shift? Appalled by the generational treadmill that saw his male relatives broken in one way or another by the dead-end jobs in the auto industry that provided the economic backbone of Flint, Michigan, Ben Hamper longs to escape a similar fate.

After an adolescence spent goofing off on booze and soft drugs to a soundtrack of acid rock and punk, Hamper inevitably finds himself consigned to the land that time-and-a-half forgot. Railing against the desolate tedium of assembly line tasks, Hamper seeks to beat the clock. Finding sharp partners amongst the lumpen cruds that populate the factory floor, Hamper and his friends double-up tasks to dodge work, enabling illicit temporary escapes from the assembly line to drink at nearby bars. Meanwhile, the management dreams up absurd schemes to motivate their apathetic workforce: a grown man haunts the factory dressed as Howie Makem, the 'Quality Cat'. Faced with such incentives, the only sane response is madness. To kill time, Hamper and his misanthropic mate Dave Steel devise a film scenario entitled ***No Need For The Grievance Procedure***, in which their despised foreman is playfully eliminated.

Anyone who has toiled in a factory (as this author once did) will immediately relate to the reality of the blue-collar experience Hamper rampantly describes. Those lucky enough never to have held a manufacturing job will also be wildly amused by Hamper's mildly dysfunctional (yet utterly unexaggerated) tales. A classic of black humour, uproarious laughter simply tumbles from the pages of ***Rivethead***.

Hamper's notoriety began when he started writing about his work for a local newspaper, attracting the attention of journalist Michael Moore, who readily collaborated with The Rivethead before producing a string of polemical left-wing documentary films and TV shows. The kind of guy who is happy to visit Manhattan drugstores asking for condoms in size 'small' while the escapade is filmed with a hidden camera, Ben Hamper is a bigger hero to real men than all those CEOs will ever be.

Read on

Don't talk to me about work: George Orwell, *Down and Out in Paris and London* (NF); Alan Sillitoe, *Saturday Night and Sunday Morning*; Upton Sinclair, *The Jungle*; H.G. Wells, *The History of Mr Polly*; Emile Zola, *Germinal*

M. JOHN HARRISON (b. 1945) UK

CLIMBERS (1989)

It's been said that men have hobbies instead of emotions. The pastimes we choose help us examine and express our feelings in ways so subtle that women cannot comprehend them, and that even men themselves struggle to put into words. Luckily, we have writers like M. John Harrison to embody the spirit of our interests for us.

Mike escapes from his relationship with Pauline by leaving London and moving north. In Manchester he is closer to the cliffs of Yorkshire and North Wales. In the company of a diverse group of men whose differences are irrelevant in the face of their fixation on scaling sheer mountainsides, Mike finds a species of purity and glimpses the meaning of freedom. When one is high above the ground and in the instant, it doesn't matter that one of the group is a teacher while another is a butcher's boy. Meaningless social divisions melt away, but the hazards of the men's common passion are always present. To fall out of mundane everyday existence while climbing is one thing, but to slip the noose of fate and tumble towards death is the gamble Mike and his companions must always take in pursuit of the sublime.

A man without a fascination is incomplete and stunted. *Climbers* is about the nature of obsession and how it grips us. Like all great writers Harrison shows rather than tells you why his characters adore their hobby, never spelling out the reasons, never risking the demystification of the intangible bliss we discover in our recreations. Harrison's ability as an observational writer is formidable and he is widely feted for his insights into people, places and things while his excellent prose style has turned many more commercially successful novelists green. A climber and fell-runner himself, Harrison is well known for his remarkable literary SF and fantasy. *Climbers* is his only mainstream novel and the first work of fiction to have won the Boardman Tasker mountaineering literature prize. No particular curiosity for the sport is necessary for any man to enjoy *Climbers* – no matter what your own hobby is, this is a book for you.

See also: *100 Must-Read Science Fiction Novels*

Read on

Things That Never Happen (contains the stories 'The Ice Monkey' and 'Egnaro', which echo elements of *Climbers*)

›› Garry Kilworth, *The Songbirds of Pain*; Keith Roberts, *The Chalk Giants*; ›› James Salter, *Solo Faces*; Alan Sillitoe, *The Loneliness of the Long Distance Runner*

ERNEST HEMINGWAY (1899–1961) USA

ISLANDS IN THE STREAM (1970)

A posthumously published tripartite novel whose separate elements typify Hemingway's ruggedly masculine output, *Islands in the Stream* includes all of the author's classic themes and subjects.

The first segment of the book concerns Thomas Hudson, a painter and one-time friend of James Joyce dwelling amongst other artists, boozers and scrappers on an idyllic Gulf Stream island. A moving tale of coming of age through the medium of deep-sea fishing, and of a father bonding intensely with his visiting sons, it is furnished with an incredibly heart-rending conclusion. The second part finds the protagonist in Cuba surrounded by cats, dogs and an array of royals, soldiers and locals as World War II rages on elsewhere. There is reconciliation with an ex-wife, but also a further instance of tremendous sadness. In the concluding third, Hudson has joined the war effort as captain of a little boat, eager for contact with elusive Germans.

A friend of this author once described Hemingway as a drinkin', fishin', shootin', shaggin' writer and I still can't fault this analysis. His novels and stories are wrenched from the rich earth, screaming out their rough-edged authenticity, and he is proof not only that real men do read books, but that they write them as well. Nevertheless, in this quietly elegiac final novel there is evidence both of tenderness and humour: oft-ignored qualities in Hemingway's writing.

Rebellion against a soft Protestant upbringing was almost certainly instrumental in forming 'Papa' Hemingway's tough outdoorsman character, which is reflected in countless memorable characters, as are his rocky relationships with women. He flung himself into various conflicts with great ardour when the opportunity arose (albeit mainly from a journalistic standpoint) and was a champion of the loyalist cause during the Spanish Civil War. Suicidal tendencies claimed the lives of many of Hemingway's relatives and he succumbed to a self-administered shotgun blast when medication deprived him of his creative faculties.

See also: *100 Must-Read Classic Novels*

Film version: *Islands in the Stream* (1977)

Read on

The Old Man and the Sea; *A Farewell to Arms*; *Men Without Women*; *Death in the Afternoon* (NF)

W. Somerset Maugham, *The Moon and Sixpence*

HERMANN HESSE (1877–1962) Germany

STEPPENWOLF (1927)

Henry Haller is a fiftyish freethinker who resides in a rented apartment. Out of sorts with his fellow man, Haller likens himself to a lone lupine that strays from the wilderness into a city, dubbing himself the Steppenwolf. Spending his days in solitude reading poetry and philosophy, sipping cherry brandy and taking solitary walks, Haller has lost all his passion for living, enthused only by the pleasures of the intellect.

One night Haller takes a stroll in the darkest part of the town. Passing alongside an old wall he spies an archway he has not previously noticed. A flashing neon sign surmounts the heavy door set in the arch, its reflection dancing on the wetness of the road. The legend reads 'Magic Theatre! Entrance not for everybody'. After failing to open the door, Haller steps back and the neon pulses another message at him: 'For Madmen Only!'. When the Steppenwolf finally gains admission to the venue behind the mysterious portal he will find himself re-admitted to a garden of sensual delights and experiences he believed were lost to him forever with his vanished youth.

Like Tolkien, Nobel prizewinner Hesse found a mass audience in the sixties when Western youth discovered the poetic elements of his work that they interpreted as psychedelic. One rock band took the title of his most famous book as their name, their anthem 'Born To Be Wild' appearing in quintessential hippy film ***Easy Rider***, while another (Hawkwind) recorded a song entitled Steppenwolf, their singer Robert Calvert (himself a poet and novelist who suffered from manic despression) dressing as Haller onstage and re-enacting the man-wolf's misanthropic agonies.

Combining Modernism with German Romanticism, Hesse was one of the finest proponents of the *Bildungsroman*, the novel form that reveals a man's journey through life and the influences of elder mentors upon him, penning several poignant books that dexterously examined the relationships between men. In *Steppenwolf*, an affirming read that does not insult the intelligence, he inspirationally encourages both the young and the middle-aged to subdue their angst and appreciate existence for its own sake.

See also: *100 Must-Read Life-Changing Books*

Film version: *Steppenwolf* (1974)

Read on

Demain; *The Glass Bead Game* (aka *Magister Ludi*)

Loners: Samuel Beckett, *The Expelled*; Knut Hamsun, *Hunger*; John Williams, *Stoner*

PATRICIA HIGHSMITH (1921–95) USA

RIPLEY UNDER GROUND (1970)

Some years after he manslaughters a rich friend and forges his will to name himself as sole beneficiary, sensitive psychopath Tom Ripley is residing comfortably in a French villa. Having left the gaucheness of his youth behind him, Tom has married the wealthy, blonde Heloise and spends his days at leisure, gardening, reading and learning languages.

The bourgeois routine of Tom's luxurious existence is overturned by the news that an American art collector called Murchison is expressing doubts about the authenticity of a painting he acquired from a London gallery Tom has shares in. Tom and his partners have no little cause for concern when Murchison announces he wants to consult an expert opinion, for the latter is correct: maestro modernist Derwatt died in secret years earlier, the gallery has commissioning fakes for some time. To prevent the fraud from being exposed, Tom takes the audacious step of impersonating Derwatt at a press conference. But Murchison isn't shaken off so easily and Tom is forced to improvise as the web of deceit the gallery has spun becomes more convoluted and restrictive. Tom is a pleasant man, but should it be expedient to murder Murchison to preserve the status quo, he will be nothing loath.

Although a marvellous novel in itself, ***The Talented Mr Ripley*** can be seen as an insightful prologue to Patricia Highsmith's idiosyncratic series of thrillers. ***Ripley Under Ground*** sees the shocking escapades of the charming killer slide into high gear. The considerable risks Ripley takes to defend his lifestyle dizzy the reader into submission and once the novel is over one cannot help clamouring for more of this disarmingly chameleonic villain.

The oddly seductive nature of Tom Ripley's cosmopolitan character is partially explained by his creator's history: an American who spent much of her life in Europe, Patricia Highsmith was a bisexual and alcoholic who endured a number of tempestuous relationships. Highsmith's gender identity, rapacious wit and stature as the most eminent suspense writer of her times reflects Ripley's place as the most likeable crook in the annals of literature. All the best people have thoroughly enjoyed Tom's company and there is no reasonable excuse for not being part of his circle.

Film version: *Ripley Under Ground* (2005)
Sequels: *Ripley's Game*; *The Boy Who Followed Ripley*; *Ripley Under Water*
Read on
Strangers on a Train; *Found in the Street*

ANTHONY HOPE (1863–1933) UK

THE PRISONER OF ZENDA (1894)

The Prisoner of Zenda is a picaresque extravaganza centring upon the uncanny resemblance between rich English idler Rudolph Rassendyll and the future king of Ruritania, an imaginary European nation.

Stung by accusations of inertia, Rassendyll decides to attend the coronation of King Rudolph V (Elphberg) in the land where his own family is said to have a line of ancestry. There he hopes to research a book on Ruritanian political history, although the volume he ends up writing is a far more flavoursome affair. He arrives in the town of Zenda, where Black Michael (who covets the throne) has his castle and enjoys much local support. Rudolph soon meets his namesake, who turns out to be virtually his double. They immediately become firm friends and the king drinks himself into a stupor. Unfortunately, the wine was a gift from Black Michael and is drugged so, consequently, Elphberg is in no state to attend his own coronation the following day. This being fiction, the only avenue considered is the most exciting. Rassendyll will impersonate the sovereign and be 'crowned' in his stead.

Our hero plays his part well until he meets the king's intended bride and begins to court her with an ardour beyond that of his regal counterpart. Furthermore, he returns to find Elphberg missing, transported to Michael's castle a prisoner. There is now no option but for Rassendyll to keep up his charade until a rescue plot can be hatched.

Hope's swashbuckling novella was an instant commercial success and allowed him to give up a legal career to pursue the literary life. Hallmarks of the classic escapist romp such as love, subterfuge and swordplay mesh irresistibly in this tightly written, pacy package that sits comfortably in the tradition of Dumas and all the very best boy's own-style ripping yarns.

Film versions: (all eponymous) 1913, 1922, 1937, 1952, 1979
Sequel: *Rupert of Hentzau*
Read on
John Buchan, ***Mr Standfast***; Erskine Childers, ***The Riddle of the Sands***; Alexandre Dumas, ***The Man in the Iron Mask***; Philip Jose Farmer, ***Greatheart Silver***

ROBERT E. HOWARD (1906–36) USA

THE COMPLETE CHRONICLES OF CONAN

(Centenary Edition, collected 2006)

Two reavers wielding broadswords stand off across a freezing battlefield bathed in sunlight and spattered with the gore of myriads of fallen warriors. Within seconds, one is dead. The victor is the mightily thewed Conan, a mercenary and thief from the harsh province of

Cimmeria. Dizzied by hours of fighting, the savage barbarian sinks to his knees. Then the mocking quicksilver laughter of a girl rings in his ears.

Looking up in surprise, Conan beholds a comely maiden standing before him. Naked apart from a gossamer wrap, the girl's fulsome, immaculate body is like marble, her glorious tresses ablaze, her eyes rippling with oceanic hues. Taunting the exhausted swordsman that he is only fit to lie down and die when a real man would ravish her, the girl mocks him. Despite his fatigue, Conan's blood is up and he only has rape in mind. But in the ancient world of Hyperborea, soldiers of fortune must tread carefully, as eerie forces wait to destroy those who lower their guard.

The adventures of Conan the Barbarian started appearing in 1932. 'The Frost Giant's Daughter' is just one of the tales that comprise the definitive edition of these seminal works of the heroic fantasy genre. Predating Tolkien while admitting the influence of Burroughs, Howard fundamentally created Sword and Sorcery as we know it. Lusty and vibrant, Conan is a manly, ale-swilling rough-houser oftimes at odds with blackguardly wizards, forever carousing with voluptuous Amazons, inhabiting a detailed fictional world that has never needed supplemental volumes of appendixes to make it convincing.

Howard's sinewy prose may be a prime example of pulp excess, but it is not without flashes of poetry that illuminate the beserker fury of his stirring narratives. Conan remains the only worthwhile companion for those moments when the urge to grow your beard, don a horned helmet and quaff innumerable pitchers of lager is strong in you. An essential addition to any masculine library, we recommend you invest in the black faux-leather hardback edition of this protean 900-page volume.

Film version: *Conan The Barbarian* (1981)

Read on

Blood and thunder: Poul Anderson, ***The Broken Sword***; Edgar Rice Burroughs, ***Tarzan of the Apes***; Fritz Leiber, ***Swords Against Deviltry*** (aka ***The First Book of Lankhmar***); Michael Moorcock, ***Elric of Melnibone***; Michael Shea, ***The Incompleat Nifft***

READ ON A THEME: ROMAN

There are so many unmissable Roman Empire novels, we couldn't choose just one. So here we flying the standard for the very best sword and sandal fiction based on historical events:

Gillian Bradshaw, ***Island of Ghosts*** – Roman cavalry battles the Picts

Wallace Breem, ***Eagle in the Snow*** – defending the frontier against the Barbarians

Ralph Graves, ***The Lost Eagles*** – the recovery of lost legionary standards in Germania

Robert Graves, ***I, Claudius***; ***Claudius The God*** – the definitive imperial dynasty diptych

Robert Harris, ***Pompeii*** – drama in the celebrated city beside Vesuvius

Andrew Quiller, ***The Eagles Series*** (***The Hill of the Dead***; ***The Land of Mist***; ***City of Fire***; ***Blood on the Sand***; ***Sea of Swords***) – the ultimate gladiatorial epic

Keith Roberts, *The Boat of Fate* – depicting the cosmopolitan sweep of the Empire
George Shipway, *Imperial Governor* – the Boudician Revolt of AD 60

SIMON HUGHES (b. 1959) UK

A LOT OF HARD YAKKA (1997) (NF)

Simon Hughes may be at pains to stress his mediocrity as a human being, but not many people get to play sport for a living, so he must have a certain amount of talent. That talent extended to a career in television commentary and the production of one of the most riveting sporting reads published. ***A Lot of Hard Yakka*** succeeds despite the fact that (or perhaps because) it is about workaday domestic cricket rather than Ashes campaigns or England being decimated by West Indian fast bowling.

Recruited by Middlesex in 1980, Hughes is struck by the lascivious banter and slack training methods he encounters while gaining impressions of international players such as Mike Gatting and the expletive-laden John Emburey. Then there is the partially sighted old physiotherapist, the hopeless posh kid who got into the squad because of his dad's connections, and of course the legends – Botham, Richard Hadlee and Co – each described with unrelentingly subjective honesty. Hughes reveals batsmen's various reactions to being dismissed, their eating habits and changing room rituals, the verbal abuse and the high-jinks, and it is his genius for pinpointing character traits which elevates the book to the level of sporting classic.

Hughes is no politician and makes the odd unconscious generalisation whilst upbraiding others for their backward opinions, but he is always warm-hearted and his wide-eyed wonder at the not-so-middle-class realm of the county circuit is endearing. Never an England player, it was a decade before he came to regret not pressing home his advantage when offered a pre-tour trial but, as we all know, socialising often comes first when you are young.

Sequels: *Yakking Around the World* (NF); *Morning Everyone* (NF)

Read on

Marcus Berkmann, ***Rain Men*** (NF); David English, ***Mad Dogs and the Englishman*** (NF); Hugh de Selincourt, ***The Cricket Match***; Ed Smith, ***On and Off the Field*** (NF)

JORIS-KARL HUYSMANS (1848–1907) France

A REBOURS (AGAINST NATURE) (1884)

Des Esseintes is an epicurean libertine eternally seeking new and exclusive thrills. Purchasing a house he decorates it according to eccentric themes so as to fuel his flaccid imagination. Consequently, he manages to avoid unnecessary contact with the human beings he so despises. Esseintes appeals partly to the feminine or foppish side of man yet he is also the equivalent of a contemporary guy with cash to burn, kitting out his pad according to a lads' ideal with the latest sound and vision systems (a man's home is his castle and all that). Instead, Huysmans' hero has bookshelves lined with carefully chosen works of decadent and free-thinking literature, walls hung with peculiar and grotesque art, and the most exotic plants cascading through his domain. Attempting to temper the garishness of his carpet, he allows a jewel-encrusted tortoise to plod around on it but the creature expires from the excitement of it all.

The *pièce de résistance* is what Des Esseintes calls his mouth organ: a wondrous contraption that dispenses liqueurs with which he plays symphonies on his tongue, a drop of this, a sip of that, each flavour corresponding to the distinct voice of an instrument. The phantasmagoric effects of his surroundings trigger menacing, supernatural dreams and a worsening sickness and depression. Evocations of his past rain down on him and he reminisces about times when he has toyed with the lives of others, revelling in the misfortune and damage to their characters he has caused. He reflects on his inherited Christianity, which (apart from sporadic bouts of piety) holds scant appeal, lamenting the physical and sexual inadequacies with which he is cursed.

Parisian Huysmans' life was distinctly ordinary. His books are quite the opposite: a partial rebellion against Zola's naturalistic vision of literature. Sinister decadence, infamous desires and immense gothic structures are his hallmarks and he indulges in the grossest of wish fulfilment, picturing himself as the depraved protagonist in several books. Any man ever involved with youth subcultures like punk and psychedelia will immediately find a kindred spirit in Des Esseintes.

Read on

La Bas aka *Down There*

Charles Baudelaire, *Les Fleurs du Mal* (poetry); J.A. Barbey d'Aurevilly, *Les Diaboliques*; Edgar Allen Poe, *Tales of Mystery and Imagination*; Patrick Suskind, *Perfume*

M.R. JAMES (1862–1936) UK

CASTING THE RUNES AND OTHER GHOST STORIES (Collected 1987)

You've been on a long hike over difficult terrain in abominable weather. Almost wet through, you gratefully stumble upon a classic British country inn. Once inside, you purchase a pint of nutty ale and blissfully sink into a chesterfield beside the roaring fire. All you need now is someone to tell you a ghost story. Wishing you could don a burgundy velvet smoking jacket, you crack a paperback by M.R. James.

The Professor is a staid and fussy old man wrapped up in woolly academic musings. Staying in a seaside lodging house during a holiday, he plays some golf with a Colonel Wilson on the links. Wandering away from his vanquished adversary, The Professor stumbles upon a site he theorises is the base of an altar. Rooting about with his penknife, he unearths an ancient whistle bearing a Latin inscription punctuated by swastikas. Back in his room, he translates the legend as 'Who is this who is coming?'. Thoughtlessly blowing on the tiny instrument, The Professor does not suspect that something will heed the reedy siren call of the relic ...

'Oh, Whistle, and I'll Come to You, My Lad' is one of the most celebrated ghost stories in the English language. This essential collection contains 29 other sterling supernatural tales, including masterworks as 'A Warning To The Curious' and 'Casting The Runes' (possibly an Aleister Crowley tribute). Extremely stylised and genteel, the sheer Englishness of James' perennial settings and protagonists – public schools, churches, antiquarians, lecturers and clergymen – is both utterly charming and highly addictive. But the comforting parochial backdrops of James' eldritch yarns are deceptive, contrasting wonderfully with the chilling spectral terror he conjures.

Provost of King's College Cambridge, James' studious life was reflected in his fiction. A respected Medievalist, he will always be remembered as the unmatched Grandmaster of Ghouls. His elegant amusements will have you casting nervous glances over your shoulder in an ecstasy of shudders.

☐ **TV plays:** numerous James stories have been filmed for television. *Whistle and I'll Come To You* (1968); *A Warning To The Curious* (1972) and *Casting The Runes* (1978) have appeared on DVD.

Read on

Haunted men: J. Sheridan Le Fanu, *In A Glass Darkly*; M. John Harrison, *The Ice Monkey*; Richard Matheson, *Hell House*; Oliver Onions, *The Beckoning Fair One*; Colin Wilson, *Poltergeist* (NF)

GARRY KILWORTH (b. 1941) UK

WITCHWATER COUNTRY (1986)

Titch Swan lives with his grandparents in the marshlands of rural Essex. Enjoying all the boyhood excitements a rustic 1950s upbringing can offer, Titch and three friends spend their summer holidays playing war games, skinny dipping and frightening each other with stories of the old woman who lives in the white clapperboard house beside a shadowy pond. In their local mythology, she is a Water Witch, an evil crone bent on the destruction of small boys.

Poaching with his roguish Uncle Dave, continually asking his Grandad how he lost his leg in the Great War and always receiving a different reply, reading H.G. Wells and listening to ***The Man in Black*** on the radio, it seems as if Titch's childhood will never end. But when one of his chums apparently drowns as the result of a dare set by a local girl, Titch begins to realise that the self-imposed scares of his boyish imagination are as nothing compared to the real darkness that confronts him as he begins to mature into a man.

Son of an airman, Garry Kilworth grew up in Arabia, later joining the RAF himself before beginning his literary career as an SF writer in the 1970s. He started dabbling in horror and general fiction in the 1980s and has continued to diversify ever since. Taking the Essex background of his family and splashing it with a tincture of terror, ***Witchwater Country*** is Kilworth's most satisfying novel, paying homage to Ray Bradbury's coming-of-age masterpiece ***Dandelion Wine***, another beautifully realised chronicle of a boy's transformation into an adolescent over the course of a summer clouded with superstition.

Kilworth's unsentimental yet emotive descriptions of the cruelties and bliss of boyhood will encourage many readers to recall the wonder of their own youth and question if their own children's imaginations are under-stimulated as a result of spending too little time amidst the great outdoors.

Read on

Spiral Winds; (as Garry Douglas) ***Soldiers in the Mist***
Ray Bradbury, ***Something Wicked This Way Comes***; David Mitchell, *Black Swan Green*; ›› Colin Wilson, ***The World of Violence***

JOHN KING (b. 1960) UK

THE FOOTBALL FACTORY (1996)

Rogue Chelsea fans gather for the next home game. Pre-match shags are curtailed to preserve energy for the real buzz – the fighting, which, much more than the result, will decide the success or failure of the weekend. Grudgingly respectful of Millwall and West Ham's firms, racist except when there's a black guy in their ranks, these hooligans play by vicious rules but rules nonetheless. But these thugs aren't stupid: they don't wear team strips, don't get too drunk before a ruck, don't fight in the stadium. They creep under the police radar and kick off at less conspicuous venues (tube station or High Street), but in reality, they're praying for police intervention so they can have a pop at the real enemy. They're not out to kill – most of the time – but to assert their tribal identity (team, race, gender) in a ritual, a violent contest, the anticipation of which gets them through the vacuum of each working week.

Contrary to the views of television pundits, such characters *are* football fans, albeit a deeply unpleasant minority and King adds depth to the usual news footage of barbaric clashes, putting the mayhem in its cultural context of broken families, low expectations, surveillance cameras and a justice system which working class whites do not feel represented by. The facts represented in the book are carefully selected and King slips in extraneous characters to illustrate debatable political points, but he does not deny the real reason for the aggro – that the antagonists bloody love it. King undoubtedly found the pulse of his subject matter and ***The Football Factory*** is the touchstone for all football fiction. The writing comes at you in a fluent yet frenetic torrent, drawing you into the beer-rush, thumping and pumping with the sound of an adrenaline junky's battle cry. If a post-match curry is a tactical training exercise (who to wind up, who to steer clear of, how to avoid paying) then West Ham at home is war.

Film version: *The Football Factory* (2004)

Read on

Headhunters; *England Away*

Nick Hornby, *Fever Pitch* (NF); Kevin Sampson, *Awaydays*; Colin Ward, *Steaming In* (NF);

KLAUS KINSKI (1926–91) b. Poland, Germany

KINSKI UNCUT (1991) (NF)

Most cinema buffs remember Kinski as the short-tempered, china-blue eyed hunchback outlaw called Wild in the spaghetti western *For A Few Dollars More*. Director Sergio Leone said that Kinski didn't act the part, he merely played himself instead – for in real life Kinski was very like the rabid character he was portraying. A man of tremendous passions (or very little self-control and an excess of ego), the elemental thespian always seemed to be teetering on the brink of boiling over into volcanic rage. *Kinski Uncut* furiously reveals the off-the-chain attitude and insatiable desires of this greatest of cult actors. Getting an unexpurgated version of the book into print was quite a struggle even in the liberal nineties.

After a penurious childhood in Poland, Kinski relocates to Berlin, where he is conscripted into the Wehrmacht. He develops an interest in the theatre, delivering monologues of poetry and Biblical texts – which last for hours – brilliantly delivered and received with endless standing ovations from packed houses. Caring only about his loved ones and the stage, he accepts parts in all kinds of movies indifferent to the results. Throughout his meteoric career, he garners monumental accolades from all quarters. He is also eternally besotted with sex, claiming to have rutted with virtually every woman he ever encountered, describing his conquests in blazing, expletive-ridden fervour.

Or did he? Lies and exaggeration come naturally to an actor. His superb collaborations with Werner Herzog were famously fraught with dangerous showdowns – during the shooting of *Aguirre* (which is like *Apocalypse Now* with conquistadores), star and director both spoke seriously of plotting the other's murder. But while Herzog later claimed they were winding the rest of the world up with these capers, the intensity of the latter's performances (from Dracula in ***Nosferatu*** to the stressed-out soldier ***Woyzeck***) alter the viewer's life forever. As a shameless confession of a man who allowed himself to be dominated by his lusts ***Kinski Uncut*** does the same. The reader is left wondering if a man really should live his life so aggressively, while cursing himself for his weakness in not expressing his appetites as forthrightly as this unique artiste.

Read on

Kinski's roles: George Buchner, ***Woyzek*** (drama); Bruce Chatwin, ***The Viceroy of Ouidah***

Errol Flynn, ***My Wicked Wicked Ways*** (NF); Richard E. Grant, ***With Nails*** (NF); Wernor Herzog, ***Herzog On Herzog*** (NF)

DEKE LEONARD (b. 1944) UK

WINOS, RHINOS AND LUNATICS (1996) (NF)

In 1968, The Bystanders were the top rock group in South Wales, with a record contract and a tour diary chock-full of gigs all over Britain. Meanwhile, believing that his life was utterly meaningless until he could cut at least one record, Llanelli-based guitarist Deke Leonard yearned for vinyl immortality. Asked by The Bystanders to join their ranks, the ecstatic Leonard was shocked to discover that the group was not only changing their name to Man, but were adopting a new repertoire of numbers based on free-form psychedelic jamming. Awed by the impressive chops of Micky Jones, the diminutive axeman whose incandescent mastery of the batwing Gibson SG was to remain the only constant factor in the ever-shifting line-ups of the band, Leonard rose to the challenge with an ever-present cheeky quip on his lips and lashings of mojo in his soul.

Many groups have noticed staggering parallels between the popular fictional 'rockumentary' comedy film ***This is Spinal Tap*** and their own wayward careers. Leonard hysterically reveals the minutiae of making overblown, oddly-titled albums while heroically avoiding the stigma of hit singles and wallowing in the joys of being big in Germany, unrepentantly recalling the rewards of unfeasible amounts of uncomplicated sex and numerous recreational drugs. Forever scheming with his perfectionist foil Micky Jones, Leonard conspires in the firing and hiring of the many characterful musicians who are called and get up to do their duty in the quest for the ideal Man sound.

Filled with sharp Cymric wit, ***Rhinos, Winos and Lunatics*** is not just an extremely funny book, but a quintessential chronicle of seventies rock that is soon to be immortalised as a feature film. Leonard effortlessly conjures up dozens of Withnailesque anecdotes that will make every armchair air-guitarist wish he had been a member of the Gower Peninsula's answer to The Quicksilver Messenger Service.

Read on

Prequel: *Maybe I should have stayed in bed: the flip side of the rock and roll dream* (NF); *The Twang Dynasty* (NF)

Rock follies (all NF): John Cale, ***What's Welsh For Zen***; Deborah Curtis,

Touching From A Distance: Ian Curtis and Joy Division; Ian Hunter, *Diary of a Rock 'n' Roll Star*; James Young, *Nico: Songs They Never Play on the Radio*

READ ON A THEME: MUSICIAN

Brilliant books by and about rockers

Iain Banks, *Espedair Street*
Michael Bruce, *No More Mr Nice Guy: The Inside Story of the Alice Cooper Group* (NF)
Robert Calvert, *Hype*
Hugh Cornwell, *A Multitude of Sins* (NF)
Harlan Ellison, *Spider Kiss*
Richard Hell, *Go Now*
Will Hodgkinson, *Guitar Man* (NF)
Seb Hunter, *Hell Bent For Leather* (NF)
Toby Litt, *I Play The Drums in a Band Called Okay*
Michael Moynihan and Didrik Soderlind, *Lords of Chaos: The Bloody Rise of the Satanic Metal Underground* (NF)
Lee Ranaldo, *Jrnls80s* (NF)

TED LEWIS (1940–82) UK

JACK'S RETURN HOME (aka GET CARTER) (1970)

When London-based heavy Jack Carter returns to his home town for his brother's funeral, he can't help but be suspicious: after all, Frank had always been the quiet type, never drank spirits, yet he apparently died at the wheel of his car stinking of whiskey. Not only that, but Jack has already been gently warned off interfering with their connections in the north by his bosses, the Fletcher twins, kingpins of a crime firm that runs most of the scams in the West End. But Jack is as independent as he is hard: leaving no scumbag unturned, Carter uses every violent tactic in his arsenal of intimidation to discover who Frank fell foul of and why.

As the landmark film featuring Michael Caine is well known, we won't detail the plot any further here. While the first person narrative of the novel reveals the depths of Carter's blood-thicker-than water feelings more nakedly than the film, the screen adaptation is very faithful to the book. Despite this, Lewis' brilliant novel still demands to be read. From its repulsive characters (seedy porno-loop peddlers and common-as-muck slags) to its gritty Northern setting (Scunthorpe according to one of its prequels, not Doncaster as the jacket blurbs of some recent editions have mistakenly claimed), the book's terse brutality will attract every man who has ever wanted to growl 'Shut it,' with impunity.

The powerhouse directness of the writing is impeccable, while the plotting should be used as a textbook example of storytelling perfection in creative writing classes, as it is constructed with immense precision, like a piece of fine dovetail marquetry – every single character in the book is of vital importance to the plot.

Lewis hailed from Manchester, the setting for the *Get Carter*-influenced TV series *Life On Mars*. After attending art school he worked as an animator, notably on *Yellow Submarine*. His other novels included two inferior-by-comparison (yet nevertheless excellent) prequels to *Jack's Return Home*, which remains the finest British hardboiled crime novel to date. Dying tragically young, Lewis still has few peers as one of the few UK writers able to match the authentic, stripped-down existentialism of the great American noir writers.

Film version: *Get Carter* (1971)
Read on
Prequels: *Jack Carter's Law*; *Jack Carter and the Mafia Pigeon*
Other recommended Lewis: *GBH*
Grubby gangsters: Jake Arnott, *The Long Firm*; Michael Frewin, *London Blues*

JACK LONDON (1876–1916) USA

Jack London's life is the stuff of legend. Born into poverty in Oakland, California, London pulled himself out of the gutter by his bootstraps. By the time he died, he was the most commercially successful author in the world. In the space of forty years, London was a factory worker, oyster pirate, seal hunter, hobo, goldminer, journalist and novelist. A self-educated socialist who believed in the survival of the fittest, London had a magnificent body and a passionate mind. He invented sports writing as we know it, introduced surfing to the West Coast and produced unforgettable reportage about such events as the San Francisco earthquake of 1906. If Nietzsche had ever met London, there is little doubt he would have admitted the latter was a Superman.

THE CALL OF THE WILD (1903)

1897: the gold rush is on and Buck – a St Bernard sheepdog cross – is purloined from his comfortable Southern home and sold into the bondage of a sled team. Under the dominion of lash and club, the Aurora Borealis swirling in the skies of the Yukon above him, the dog learns the primordial law that might is right. Passing from one master to another, Buck endures both cruelty and kindness, while his previously dormant instincts awaken powerfully to deal with pack rivalries. Besting the other canines in his team, the thirst for freedom swells within him. Intrigued by the feral, scrawny red-eyed curs that lurk unchained in the darkness beyond the campfires, Buck rises inexorably to the apotheosis of his innate savagery when the hour of the wolf is at hand.

Everyone thinks they know *The Call of the Wild* – it's a book for kids. Think again – for all its purple melodrama, Jack London's bestseller is one of the most sustained and unremitting depictions of brutality, humiliation and bloodletting ever committed to paper. Based on London's own experiences in the Klondike and expressing his symbolic adoption of the wolf as a personal emblem signifying his status as an independent man of action, *The Call of the Wild* is exhilarating in its worship of the hardness and beauty of raw nature.

All men who have known the unconditional faithfulness a canine companion offers pity those who have never formed such a fundamental bond. The intimate relationship between man and dog stretches back countless millennia, born of the mutual respect of fellow hunters relying on each other for survival. Some critics accuse London of excessive anthropomorphism, but recent research indicates that many higher mammals experience emotions in a very similar way to ourselves, no surprise to anyone who admires animals. In *The Call of the Wild* London captures the very essence of adventure – the moment when love of life puts his protagonist so firmly in the moment that he denies the death he knows is only a hair's breadth away.

Thematic sequel: *White Fang*
Significant film versions: (all eponymous) 1923, 1935, 1975
Read on
Love of Life
Man's best friend (all NF): Benedict Allen, *Into The Abyss*; J. Percy Fitzpatrick, *Jock of the Bushveld*; Fred Gipson, *Old Yeller*; Gary Paulsen, *Winterdance*

JOHN BARLEYCORN (1913) (NF)

Few of us enjoy our first sips of beer, wine or spirits. As boys when we ask our fathers how they can bear to down pints, they speak of acquiring the taste and drinking to be sociable. We are baffled. Our fathers, however, are wiser than we know. Like so many men, London's early experiences of alcohol were unpleasant, but camaraderie and circumstance drew him to the iniquities of his nemesis John Barleycorn, the soul of booze. London never acquired the taste: he drank because in the manly lines of employment he pursued, to be inebriated was to be both heroic and accepted. Eventually, London could not stop drinking.

John Barleycorn is an exceptional yet criminally neglected autobiography by one of America's greatest popular writers. London warmly regales us with sparkling tales of his adventurous existence, revealing the euphoria of seafaring and prospecting darkly through a glass of rye. Expounding his beliefs energetically, he warns us of the insidious evils of alcohol. But this is a controversial book, as experts are divided about how true London's confessions are, some suggesting he was never as habitually besotted as he claims.

To have been a confidante of London must really have been something – the warmth of this freest of spirits draws the reader in and makes him feel as if he is in the man's company. Although he sometimes wrote quickly, producing prose that failed to reflect his talent, *John Barleycorn* is London at his spellbinding best, a true classic of American literature that deserves to stand alongside the works of Melville and Twain.

Read on

The Sea Wolf

Martin Eden, ***People of the Abyss*** (NF); Hamlin Garland, ***A Son of the Middle Border*** (NF); Bret Harte, ***Gold Rush*** (NF)

CORMAC McCARTHY (b. 1933) USA

THE ROAD (2006)

Civilisation has ended, the cities burned to ash, the earth blighted, the skies perpetually overcast and leaden. Billions have died. The few survivors include a man and his child, a boy born shortly after the moment of holocaust. Quietly determined that his son will reach adulthood, the man leads the boy along a south-bound blacktop. Literally starving, dressed in rags, beset by the vile nuclear winter, vigilance is the man's priority, for other survivors eke out a savage existence by sustaining themselves on the flesh of the weak. Not yet an adolescent, the boy lives in fear, never having known a better world. The man has no reason to believe their journey will terminate in anything other than death, but his stoic devotion to his son is a driving force as fierce and silent as Armageddon itself.

McCarthy generally chronicles Southern life and history, employing a dense, verbose style that leads many to compare him to Faulkner. His vocabulary is peerless, using obscure, archaic words and odd phrasing that melds vertiginously with stream of consciousness descriptions terrible in their beauty. Despite a period of crossover popularity resulting from critical acclaim for ***All The Pretty Horses*** (1992), McCarthy's following has always been profoundly male, as the majority of his novels can be broadly classed as Westerns of a unique character. ***Blood Meridian*** (1985) is one of the grimmest, most disturbing books of recent times, its unremittingly merciless and atrocity-strewn vision of the West comparable to the most extreme works of De Sade and **››** William Burroughs. In *The Road*, McCarthy employs a stripped-down style whose spareness mirrors the wordiness of his earlier books, only inserting unfamiliar terms into the text towards the end of the story, this simplicity of approach echoing the bleakness of the setting.

When writers of general literature turn to science fiction the results are often disappointing because of their failure to balance speculative concepts equally with character study. *The Road*, however, is a worthy companion for the classics of post-nuclear SF, the feral grimness of McCarthy's blasted Earth surpassed only by the father's iron resolve in protecting his son, both conveyed majestically by this Pulitzer Prize-winning genius.

Read on

No Country For Old Men

Survivors: Harlan Ellison, 'A Boy and His Dog', from ***The Beast That Shouted Love at the Heart of the World***; Pat Frank, ***Alas, Babylon***; M. John Harrison, ***The Committed Men***; George Stewart, ***Earth Abides*** (see *100 Must-Read Science Fiction Novels*)

IAN McEWAN (b. 1948) UK

A CHILD IN TIME (1987)

The title of Ian McEwan's third novel is a dead giveaway. It explores childhood in all its forms: abstract governmental theory on child development; the emergence of the inner child and the incalculable suffering of a father who loses his daughter. It also expresses the unreliability of perceived time: time spent mourning, time trapped under an overturned lorry and even a spot of time travel.

Stephen, a writer, is enjoying the success of a novel (that is regarded as a reminder to children that their youth is temporary), when his young daughter is snatched during a trip to the supermarket. *A Child in Time*'s initial premise is a parent's ultimate idea of Hell viewed from the father's perspective but it expands and metamorphoses far beyond expressions of grief. As so often happens in reality, and through no party's clear fault, the trauma drives a wedge between Stephen and his wife, and their separation gives the former an opportunity to ponder the different attitudes to life and fate held by the sexes. These considerations lead Stephen to a hallucination of his parents remonstrating with each other before he was born, a possible sighting of his lost child and an extraordinary visit to a batty old school friend who has left his post with the government to build tree-houses and play with catapults.

McEwan does dark undercurrents better than almost anyone else. Plundering the male psyche he finds surprises everywhere, as exemplified by the ghastly but wonderfully funny episode involving the lorry driver who is convinced that he is going to die after flipping his rig over in front of Stephen's oncoming car, and famously through the by-play of stalker and stalked in Enduring Love.

Read on

The Cement Garden; *Atonement*; *Saturday*
Patrick McGrath, *Spider*

NORMAN MAILER (1923–2007) USA

THE FIGHT (1975) (NF)

In reporting Muhammad Ali's historic 1974 boxing match with undefeated George Foreman in tyrannical President Mobutu's Zaire, Mailer gives us a lesson in 'more is less', sculpting a masterpiece out of next to nothing. As the clock ticks down to the famed Rumble in the Jungle, Mailer's renown as a journalist affords him privileged access to both fighters and to Ali in particular; a man wary of whites and militantly proud of his own racial heritage while paradoxically open and approachable. The quick-fire rhyming jibes of Ali and each camp's followers and promoters are a precursor to the freestyle rap of eighties New York. Mailer senses an insecurity and guardedness in Ali's bluster though, whereas Foreman has a calm, amiable authority about him (many black Americans saw Foreman as representative of an oppressive America, most people nowadays seeing him as representative of an ingenious tilting grill) but it is during Mailer's incomparable, meticulous description of the most memorable of boxing contests where the real talking is done. Mailer pays homage to Ali's unmatched speed and skill but is not afraid to comment on the boxer's reluctance to train now that he is entering the final few years of his illustrious career. He also writes candidly (in the third person) about his own racial prejudices and his despair at how the generosity of his character appeared to shrink as he aged. Part of his motivation for writing the book was to look into the hearts and souls of black people in an attempt to educate himself.

Norman Mailer was a prolific, multiple Pulitzer-winning novelist and journalist, covering such topics as the Vietnam War, the controversy of Marilyn Monroe's death and, most recently, the early life of Hitler. Seen by some as egotistical (*The Fight* is as much about Mailer as it is about his subjects), and despised by feminists for perceived attitudes towards women, he is nevertheless judged fairly to be one of the greatest writers of the past hundred years – as well as an archetypal male author to boot.

Read on

The Naked and the Dead; *The Castle in the Forest*

Fisticuffs: Donald McRae, ***Dark Trade*** (NF); David Remnick, ***King of the World*** (NF); F.X. Toole, ***Rope Burns***

DANIEL P. MANNIX (1911–97) USA

THE HELLFIRE CLUB (1959)

Once a man reaches a certain age, he finds the conduct of younger males wanting. He thinks antisocial behaviour is getting worse, but history shows us that men have always behaved badly and that delinquency is not a new phenomenon. ***The Hellfire Club*** describes the wicked antics of upper class mid-eighteenth century English rakes, all of whom should have known better than to indulge in the blind drunkenness, wanton cruelty and sexual excesses that were their favourite pastimes.

Beginning by outlining the debauched practises of London's dandies in general, the book shifts its attention to Sir Francis Dashwood, a baron and politician who founded the most notorious rake's cabal, the Hellfire Club. This exclusive gathering included some of the most powerful men in the land, who met at a specially built abbey in the grounds of

Dashwood's estate. Clad in monkish regalia, the 'brothers' held drunken orgies with whores dressed as nuns, tried their hands at black masses and rendered themselves insensible with copious amounts of wine. But it wasn't all fun and games: many of the Hellfire Club were seriously engaged in statesmanship and the arts. ***The Hellfire Club*** is an irreverent tome that probably irritates sniffy academics but insightfully illustrates the way men balance private irresponsibility with public duty.

Daniel P. Mannix worked as a big-game trapper and conjuror, but will chiefly be remembered as the grand master of sensational non-fiction in the age of pulp exploitation paperbacks, producing lurid yet convincing works on such edifying subjects as freaks, the history of torture and the barbarities of the Roman arena. His best-known books were his children's story ***The Fox and the Hound*** and the lively autobiographical recounting of his time working in a circus entitled ***Memoirs of a Sword-Swallower***.

Read on

Those About To Die aka *The Way of the Gladiator* (NF) (reportedly the basis of the film *Gladiator*)

James Landale, ***Duel: A True Story of Death and Honour*** (NF); Fergus Linnane, ***The Lives of the English Rakes*** (NF); Hallie Rubenhold, ***Harris' List of Covent Garden Ladies*** (NF)

HOWARD MARKS (b. 1945) UK

MR NICE (1996) (NF)

On arriving for signing sessions at bookshops, it is alleged that the first thing Howard Marks used to do was offer his hosts a joint. But Marks is not a monosyllabic nutcase whose memoirs are desperately ghost-written into something vaguely interesting; instead he is a smart, charming, mischievous individual and these attributes glow warmly across every page of the intriguing tale of a bloke who eschews violence and hard drugs but was at one time the most wanted man in Britain.

As breeding grounds for criminals go, Balliol College, Oxford in the late 1960s would be a reluctant contender, but that's where Marks got a taste for the dope that would soon make him an illicit fortune. Disarmingly, he describes his wrongdoings as merely transporting beneficial herbs from one place to another. His outpourings on smuggling rackets, his relationship with the IRA, the Mafia and MI6, and his subsequent seven-year acquaintance with the US penal system are jaunty and genuinely jocular.

Howard Marks campaigns to this day for the legalisation of marijuana having stood for parliament in 1997. His arguments, although familiar, are in many ways persuasive – after all, cannabis is used by doctors to alleviate the suffering of cancer patients and is a naturally occurring substance. Marks insists that dope does not invoke violent mindsets and that legalisation would save otherwise law-abiding people from arrest, pointing out that decisions to prosecute are made arbitrarily. Counter arguments regarding the long-term deterioration of many users' mental and physical health also carry weight, but Marks' insistence that it is the individual's right to make up his own mind will find many readers agreeing that the debate must continue.

Read on

The Howard Marks Book of Dope Stories (NF); *Señor Nice – Straight Stories from Wales to South America* (NF)

›› Mark Bowden, ***Killing Pablo*** (NF); Henrey De Monfried, ***Hashish: A Smuggler's Tale*** (NF); Robert Sabbag, ***Snowblind*** (NF); Phil Sparrowhawk, *Grass* (NF);

GABRIEL GARCIA MARQUEZ (b. 1927) Colombia

MEMORIES OF MY MELANCHOLY WHORES (2004)

A nonagenarian finds solace and a whisper of lost youth in the company of a fourteen-year-old prostitute provided by Mme Rosa to his exact specifications. Their assignations are carefully staged and he is ever the gentleman. Never having known the spontaneity of mutual adoration, the protagonist has paid every woman he has ever slept with, but with the girl he discovers something new – a revitalising relationship and a belated first taste of love. He writes endearingly of his feelings for the prostitute in his newspaper column (without specifying that these love letters and reflections are in her honour), and Marquez's novella manages never to plumb the depths of seediness, largely because the narrator spends most of the time watching the girl sleep whilst keeping his hands to himself. His younger work colleagues gently mock him for his foibles and flirt teasingly with him but most are secretly impressed with this vital, love-struck oldster. Certain events (such as a chance meeting with an old flame) conjure up sentimental reminiscences of a full yet in many ways dissatisfying life. In his mind, he relives a chequered past replete with romance and disappointment, companionship and vulnerability. In particular, he recalls the moment of desolation, many years past, when he realised he was no longer young, when every moment began to count and death arose as a constant spectre. As we grow older, opportunities still remain for men to find rapture, even if it is only in our memories.

Nobel prize-winner Marquez was a pioneer of magic realism, exemplified by ***One Hundred Years of Solitude***, a book that helped to legitimise fantastic fiction in the eyes of staid critics. However, the pictures he paints of South American life and corrupt politics are convincing and heartfelt, and most of his works are rooted in a more recognisable reality. He is a key figure in the global rise of South American fiction, alongside the likes of Mario Vargas Llosa and Jorge Luis Borges.

See also: *100 Must-Read Life-Changing Books*

Read on

News of a Kidnapping; *Love in the Time of Cholera*

Haruki Murakami, *The Wind Up Bird Chronicle*; Vladimir Nabokov, *Lolita*; Italo Svevo, *As A Man Grows Older*

GEORGE R.R. MARTIN (b.1948) USA

FEVRE DREAM (1982)

The Mississippi River, 1857. Abner Marsh is steamboat captain beset by misfortune, with only one ailing craft left in his fleet. Yet Marsh's renown as a pilot goes before him, and he has attracted the attention of one Joshua York, a mysterious gentleman who insists on meeting the Captain in a shady hotel at midnight. York offers to buy half shares in Abner's company and invest in building a luxury paddle-steamer. Marsh acquiesces to the proposal.

Soon the *Fevre Dream* is hailed as the grandest vessel ever to sail from St Louis to New Orleans. But Marsh is suspicious of the strange habits of his partner passenger: York's insistence on sleeping all day, his fascination with the shoreline murders that accompany the boat's voyage and the bottles of viscous wine the dandy sups indicate that something is wrong. When York reveals the true nature of his enmity with the imperious Damon Julian, a sadistic plantation owner, Marsh is horrified to discover that he has made a deal with something that is more than a man.

Combining the milieu of Mark Twain with the wrecked finery of ***Interview With The Vampire*** while homaging Bram Stoker's Renfield in the vile shape of Sour Billy, the whip-wielding overseer willing to consume human tissue in his unholy desire for immortality, ***Fevre Dream*** is a ripping yarn of the highest order. A million miles from the frilly bloodsucker romances that have exploded in the wake of ***Buffy***, this novel is a technicolour study of one man's friendship with a vampire. Especially original is Martin's use of the overweight, ugly, elderly yet courageous Marsh as a focus, a bold, refreshing answer to stereotypical action heroes.

Martin is the international bestselling author of fantasy series ***A Song of Ice and Fire***. Before this massive commercial breakthrough, he won several genre awards for science fiction stories. ***Fevre Dream***'s fusion of horror, adventure and companionship makes it one of the finest popular entertainments of the last three decades that can rightfully take its place alongside classics by H. Rider Haggard and Edgar Rice Burroughs.

Read on

Dreamsongs: A GRRM Retrospective

Philip Jose Farmer, ***The Image of the Beast***; Christopher Frayling (ed.), ***Vampyres*** (includes seminal works such as Byron's 'Fragment of a Story'); William Hjortsberg, ***Fallen Angel***; Mark Twain, ***Life on the Mississippi*** (NF)

GEORGE MELLY (1926–2007) UK

OWNING UP (1965) (NF)

Discovering Trad Jazz during his school days in the forties, George Melly retained his faith in the music throughout his time in the navy. On demob he went to work in a London art gallery for surrealist E.L.T. Mesens (another jazz buff), discovering that revivalist music was being played by a few bands around the capital. After witnessing his first jazz gig, Melly was sufficiently inspired to pursue a career as a singer.

Outrageously successful in his aim, he relished a recording career for several years before branching out into journalism and art criticism.

Owning Up is Melly's raucous recollection of hell-raising jazz band tours during the Trad boom Britain enjoyed during the fifties, when duffel-coated CND supporting beatniks sweated in cellars and provincial halls to the deafening blare of energetic ensemble musicianship. Packed with hilariously observed incident and encouragingly irresponsible characters who believed that non-conformity, eight pints of beer and a good fart were the sigils of eternal camaraderie, *Owning Up* is an autobiography that will appeal to all male readers of an iconoclastic persuasion, even if they have no interest in jazz.

With his penchant for loud striped suits, liberal views on sexuality and a cultural stance that knew few boundaries, Melly was equally comfortable as host of TV quiz show *Gallery* and as guest star on an EP by The Stranglers. A respected British eccentric, he deserves much greater recognition for his talent as a writer. *Owning Up* is quite simply one of the funniest and best-observed memoirs we have encountered. The current edition also includes Melly's other autobiographical works: *Rum, Bum and Concertina* (1977) covers his Navy days, while *Scouse Mouse* (1984) describes the singer's childhood. This omnibus paperback reproduces the books in order of internal chronology instead of in the sequence they were published, meaning that *Owning Up* forms the final section of the book. *Owning Up* is easily the highlight of the trilogy and must be read first (Melly quoted Kierkegaard's dictum that life is lived forward but understood backward as his justification for writing his autobiography in reverse). To start reading at the beginning of the omnibus edition would be overly conventional, an approach we believe George himself would have disapproved of.

Read on

Revolt Into Style (NF), *Slowing Down* (NF)
John Chilton, *Hot Jazz Warm Feet* (NF); Digby Fairweather, *George Melly: the Final Bows of a Legend* (NF); Diana Melly, *Take A Girl Like Me* (NF)

HERMAN MELVILLE (1819–91) USA

TYPEE (1846)

Maritime tales traditionally begin with by advocating life at sea; the freedom to roam, unity of like-minded men and condescension towards staid landlubbers. *Typee* begins with the narrator (Melville himself) yearning for the sight of land after six tedious months aboard a whaler, supplies depleted and romance long since drained away.

Melville submitted his autobiographical novel as wholly factual but much of this story of a man uncovering the evils of colonialism in a Polynesian paradise is drawn from the experiences of others, the better to make his point. It remains, however, a powerful portrait of man at odds with the lands of the 'savage'.

Landing at the bay of Nukuheva in 1842, the narrator is struck by the passive loathing the islanders feel for the occupying French. He determines to flee his captain's harsh regime and finds an able and enterprising companion in a fellow called Toby. Together they negotiate perilous but achingly beautiful terrain, hoping to fall in with the friendly Happars. Indeed, such is the welcome they receive they do not at first realise that it is the reputedly cannibalistic Typee tribe upon whose village they have stumbled.

The intrepid duo's experiences illuminate the injustices of the Western temperament. Americans and Europeans are easily outraged by rumours of violence visited upon sailors but choose to ignore the atrocities committed by those who ride roughshod over lives and cultures alien to them. Yet there is a dark side to the islanders and, after Toby leaves him, Melville admits to feeling that his unpredictable hosts are determined to keep him as a prisoner, albeit a pampered one.

Owing to its depth and complexity, ***Moby Dick*** (the most famous of Melville's works) was actually far less popular than ***Typee*** until well into the twentieth century. We recommend that readers tackle ***Typee*** and Melville's other seafaring novels before attempting ***Moby Dick***, because they prepare one for the difficulty of the latter and are excellent reads in themselves.

Sequels: *Omoo* (NF); *Mardi* (NF)

Read on

Redburn

Richard Henry Dana, ***Two Years Before the Mast*** (NF); Daniel Defoe, ***Robinson Crusoe***; Robert Louis Stevenson, ***The Ebb-Tide***

HENRY MILLER (1891–1980) USA

SEXUS (1949)

Philosophy meets Playboy TV in this first in a trilogy of autobiographical novels collectively entitled ***The Rosy Crucifixion***. Henry Miller is living in New York chasing a girl called Mara (among others – they all start to blend into one after a while) and scheming to get shot of his wife, Maude. He yearns for a European way of life where art and love matter more than responsibility and the daily drudgery of earning one's keep, and he has modelled his rampantly sexual lifestyle on this idealised continent of culture. Miller gives a blow-by-blow account of his romps; an explicit tour in which he highlights his tremendous staying power and inextinguishable passion whilst somehow managing to stay true to what is a fabulously written modern classic.

Alongside his transition from failed marriage to romantic satisfaction runs Miller's determination to become a writer of renown. Friends and critics make light of his pronouncements on the subject because there is no evidence that he has actually committed anything to paper. Furthermore, one fellow points out that writing is a thankless task, involving years of graft followed by years of rejection and a lifetime of public indifference. Miller needs a confidante who can appreciate his increasing *joie de vivre* and self-confident aspirations to greatness, but this is harder than it sounds. Most of his acquaintances prefer picking holes in his character and openly seducing his girlfriend, but he can hardly complain. He gives as good as he gets.

The Rosy Crucifixion is a reference to Miller's shedding of his New York persona and his rebirth as a writer in Paris. His books (many of which were, enticingly, banned in Britain and America) are a fascinating mix of fact and fancy and his characters are almost too good to be true. A cosmopolitan array of doctors, cads and lascivious housewives dance across a broad canvas; they are the gaudy brush strokes of a man whose exploits are the envy of many a plain-thinking and straight-talking bloke. Pass me a towel dear – oh, your dressing gown appears to have fallen off.

Sequels: *Plexus*; *Nexus*

Read on

Tropic of Cancer; *Tropic of Capricorn*

›› Charles Bukowski, ***Women***; Anais Nin, ***Henry and June*** (NF)

SPIKE MILLIGAN (1919–2002) b. India, UK

ADOLF HITLER: MY PART IN HIS DOWNFALL

(1971) (NF)

1939: When twenty-year old Catford resident Terence Milligan learns of the outbreak of war, he wonders if he can avoid conscription by citing groin rupture due to an ill-advised bit of weightlifting undertaken to impress a local girl with enormous breasts. Despite arguing that his injury has been exacerbated by playing the trumpet, Milligan eventually heeds his call-up notice to join the 56th Heavy Regiment Royal Artillery.

Gunner Milligan's training is interspersed with buffoonery: while the Nazi eagle spreads its wings across the Continent, our hero is busy starting a jazz band, drinking himself insensible, delivering groansome puns at every opportunity and engaging in knee-tremblers with officer's wives. His comrades-at-arms are nothing loath either, experimenting with the science of setting fire to their farts and manipulating their genitals into theatrical displays bearing titles like 'The Last Turkey in the Shop'. Milligan realises that with such sterling examples of inventiveness and verve on display, a swift, decisive victory for the British forces is assured.

The first of seven volumes of war memoirs, ***Adolf Hitler: My Part in his Downfall*** is easily one of the funniest books ever written and we warn you that your laughter will be so intense at times as to be painful. Crammed with the characteristic knack for absurdity that made Milligan the grandfather of British alternative comedy, the madcap antics of this idol of millions are as irreverent as a reader could wish for. Unforgettable caricatures of Milligan's friends and satirical observations of the preposterousness of war abound, providing evidence of seminal inspiration for the extraordinary talent who would go on to create *The Goons* and *Q*.

Although his work continues to bring joy to new generations, the war arguably sparked the famously dark side of Milligan, which manifested itself in spells of manic depression. While we thoroughly endorse the first four books in this series, readers should be aware that later volumes are less accomplished, shorter on humour and somewhat pessimistic in their meditations, revealing the tortured aspect of one of Britain's best-loved geniuses.

Sequels: (all NF) *Rommel? Gunner Who?*; *Monty – His Part in My Victory*; *Mussolini – His Part in My Downfall*; *Where Have All the Bullets Gone?*; *Goodbye Soldier*; *Peace Work*

READ ON A THEME: FUNNY MAN

Hilarious non-fiction, comedy recollections and satirical sketches

Woody Allen, *The Complete Prose*
Lenny Bruce, *How To Talk Dirty and Influence People*
Andrew Collins, *Where Did It All Go Right?: Growing Up Normal in the Seventies*
Tony Hawks, *Round Ireland With a Fridge*
Bill Hicks, *Love All the People*
P.J. O'Rourke, *The Batchelor Home Companion: A Practical Guide to Keeping House Like a Pig*
Michael Palin, *Diaries 1969–1979: The Python Years*
Vic Reeves: *Me: Moir*

YUKIO MISHIMA (1925–70) Japan

CONFESSIONS OF A MASK (translated 1958)

The child is father to the man, they say. For Yukio Mishima, one of the finest Japanese writers of the twentieth century, the discomforts of boyhood led to greater divisions in maturity. Unable to reconcile his intellectual ideals with his sado-masochistic, homo-erotic fascinations for death and night and blood, Mishima felt trapped between his flesh that was drawn toward tough masculine beauty and the traditional demands of a society bound by strict moral conventions. The struggle within Mishima reflected the tensions between pre-war Nippon and its industrial successor where emperor worship was replaced by fealty to the corporate employer. His novels mirrored these dichotomies too, often depicting the delicate social rituals of Japanese life, the concealed passions of Mishima's protagonists usually swept aside by sickening acts of violence at their denouements.

Confessions of a Mask is an autobiographical novel outlining Mishima's disorientation as he matured. Aroused by fantasies of hideous punishments meted out to immaculate male bodies, Mishima's alter ego suddenly falls in love with a beautiful girl in the final months of the Second World War. Meanwhile, his secret heart commands him to leave the factory where Zero fighters are manufactured, volunteer for Kamikaze duty and attain perfection via a youthful death. Brilliantly yet obliquely examining the interior turmoil of a youth confused about his orientation, *Confessions of a Mask* is a hard yet brittle insight into a soul in exile.

Mishima cannot be summed up by any one of his books, so our Read on list suggests the other works essential for an understanding of this disturbed genius, who was short-listed three times for the Nobel prize. A devotee of bodybuilding who believed a return to ancient Samurai ethics would reverse the spiritual decline of post-imperial Japan, Mishima finally staged a military coup accompanied by his own private army. This symbolic act of defiance inevitably failed, Mishima attempting to commit *seppuku* before being ritually beheaded by his gay lover. Epitomising the conflict between body and mind, Mishima's repulsive yet intriguing persona and writings make for compulsive reading.

Read on

Temple of the Golden Pavillion; *Runaway Horses*; *Yukio Mishima on Hagakure* (NF)

Kobo Abe, *The Face of Another*; Henry Scott Stokes, *The Life and Death of Yukio Mishima* (NF)

GRANT MORRISON (b. 1960) UK

DOOM PATROL: CRAWLING FROM THE WRECKAGE (Collected 1992) (graphic novel)

After its youngest members are killed, superhero outfit the Doom Patrol is disintegrating. One of the surviving veterans of the group is Cliff Steel, a former racing driver whose body was destroyed in a circuit crash, his brain transplanted into a mechanical physique. Tortured by phantom body syndrome, Cliff is on the brink of mental breakdown when he is introduced to Crazy Jane, a young woman so abused by her stepfather that her mind has shattered into sixty-four separate personalities, each possessing its own meta-human power. Meanwhile, Cliff's recuperating team-mate Larry (an ex-test pilot possessed by a mysterious negative energy being) absorbs a black female doctor, transforming into a hermaphroditic entity called Rebis.

Enter Niles Caulder, The Chief, paraplegic and scientific genius, long believed dead, the founding mastermind of the original Doom Patrol. Caulder beseeches the trio to resurrect the team from the ashes, to show the world that the different and the disabled can rise above their handicaps to tackle crises that ordinary heroes are unqualified to handle. When bizarre faceless beings with gigantic scissors for hands appear from nowhere, speaking in anagrams and massacring innocents at random, Cliff's instincts kick in and he leads his dysfunctional comrades into a surreal conflict that will see the unsettling, flaky personas of Crazy Jane and Rebis mesh with the cold brilliance of The Chief to confront the ultimate philosophical question: why is there something instead of nothing?

Over forty-five issues of the second run of ***Doom Patrol*** (issues 19–63 inclusive), Grant Morrison proved he was the best writer to tackle superheroes since Stan Lee. ***Crawling From the Wreckage*** collects the first six issues of this groundbreaking story arc, re-presenting the stunning opening gambit of the most intellectually satisfying comics ever published. Morrison's breathtaking command of plot, character and ideas is perfectly augmented by the incisive pencilling of artist Richard Case. Defying easy analysis, ***Doom Patrol*** is rarely mentioned in the popular press alongside better-known graphic novels because it represents the dizzying extremes of the form. Despite its avant-garde appeal, Morrison's ***Doom Patrol*** is nonetheless accessible to everyman due to the humbling stoicism and deadpan humour of Cliff Steel, a truly courageous out-of-his depth regular guy with a big problems and a bigger heart.

Sequels: *The Painting That Ate Paris*; *Down Paradise Way*; *Musclebound*; *Magic Bus*

Read on

Frank Miller et al, ***Batman: The Dark Night Returns***; Alan Moore et al, ***Watchmen***; Roy Thomas et al, ***Marvel Masterworks: X-Men Volume 6***

DAVID NOBBS (b. 1935) UK

THE DEATH OF REGINALD PERRIN (aka THE FALL AND RISE OF REGINALD PERRIN) (1975)

Reginald Iolanthe Perrin (RIP) is middle aged, middle class and in middle management. Residing in a leafy suburb, happily married to Elizabeth, Reggie commutes into London each day to his job at Sunshine Desserts. His train is always exactly eleven minutes late.

At work Reggie fantasies about having an affair with his secretary Joan, cowers before his tyrannical boss C.J. and worries that he will be left standing by thrusting young executives Tony and David, who irritatingly insist on blurting 'Great', and 'Super', in response to every bullish pronouncement C.J. utters. With his kids having flown the nest and his ability to maintain an erection despite dreams of glistening female athletes, the tedious conformity of Reggie's existence begins to get to him; one evening at dinner, he refers inadvertently to his wife's mother as 'the Hippopotamus' ...

When Elizabeth leaves Reggie alone for a few days, the strain of decades of utter conventionality transform Reggie's behaviour. Before long, he will rebel, trying to consummate his passion for Joan, mouth outrageous absurdities during a speech at the British Fruit Association and riotously insult C.J. before he finally cracks.

David Nobbs has been one of Britain's top comic authors for some forty years, consistently producing uproarious novels and television scripts of the highest quality. Although many readers will be familiar with Leonard Rossiter's magnificent portrayal of Reggie in the flawless TV series, Nobbs' novels contain unheard jokes and moments of humour then considered too black for the small screen. Fresh insights into the ridiculous, unforgettable characters and subplot arcs unfamiliar to the viewer are also to be found in the Perrin tetralogy, which ensures all of the books (even the disappointing fourth volume) are essential reading. Finally, as a telling portrait of our stressed-out working lives, *The Rise and Fall of Reginald Perrin* still provides a healthy tonic of laughter and a stinging indictment of corporate authoritarianism. It should be read immediately after you next have the urge to say 'Parsnips' to your boss.

☐ **TV series:** *The Fall and Rise of Reginald Perrin* (1976–79)
Read on
Sequels: *The Return of Reginald Perrin*; *The Better World of Reginald Perrin*; *The Legacy of Reginald Perrin*; *The Complete Pratt*
›› Peter Tinniswood, *Tales From The Long Room*

PATRICK O'BRIAN (1914–2000) UK

MASTER AND COMMANDER (1969)

1800: Jack Aubrey cannot contain his rapture at being rewarded with his first sea command but must accustom himself to the aloofness of a mostly inherited crew. Those Jack enlists to join their number include an enthusiastic young doctor, Stephen Maturin, who shares Aubrey's love of music and quickly becomes his bosom friend. Then there is Lieutenant Dillon, who has crossed paths with Maturin before, and whose discontent at his new captain's lust for prize money begins to simmer when Jack stops to secure a captured vessel rather than chasing another foe.

Some of Captain Aubrey's dilemmas are comical – what to do with a goat-buggering sailor and how to assuage his crew's supernatural fear of the resident sin eater. Others are practical – how to drill his men to achieve a decent rate of fire with the cannon. In battle the welfare of his brig (the *Sophie*) and all the men aboard hinge on his decisions, which is where O'Brian's flabbergasting depth of knowledge is revealed. Seamen's customs and language, every detail of the *Sophie*'s construction and the historical setting in which Aubrey's men sail are delivered as convincingly as if the author had lived in the early 1800s. The narrative moves along apace, never hindered or muddled by the wealth of information contained therein, the rip-roaring adventures, daring rescues and against-the-odds naval exchanges holding your attention fast. The author's dramatic sense and the underlying humour invested in his wonderfully rounded characters combine to lift the novels high above those of his competitors. O'Brian should not be judged as a genre writer as he dismissed such categorisations by producing literature of the highest order.

Born Richard Russ, O'Brian was not, as many believe, Irish (well, not very – his mother had Irish ancestors). As well as the prodigious Aubrey–Maturin series, he wrote several other titles for adults and children, and translated numerous French works, such as Henri Charriere's gritty prison chronicle *Papillon*.

Film version: *Master and Commander: The Far Side of the World* (2003)

Sequels: *Post Captain*; *HMS Surprise*; *The Mauritius Command*; *Desolation Island*; *The Fortune of War*; *The Surgeon's Mate*; *The Ionian Mission*; *Treason's Harbour*; *The Far Side of the World*; *The*

Reverse of the Medal; *The Letter of Marque*; *The Thirteen-Gun Salute*; *The Nutmeg of Consolation*; *Clarissa Oakes*; *The Wine-Dark Sea*; *The Commodore*; *The Yellow Admiral*; *The Hundred Days*; *Blue at the Mizzen*; *The Final Unfinished Voyage of Jack Aubrey*

Read on

Captain Frederick Marryat, ***Frank Mildmay***; Victor Hugo, ***Ninety-Three***; C.S. Forester, ***Mr Midshipman Hornblower***; Lothar-Gunther Buchheim, ***Das Boot***

GEORGE ORWELL (1903–50) b. India, UK

COMING UP FOR AIR (1939)

George Bowling is a portly salesman with false teeth. Fed up with his wife and kids, bored with his semi-detached house, irked by the pressures of his job, George is over the honeymoon period when it comes to domesticity. Like thousands of other men dissatisfied with his lot, George is realistic enough to understand that dreaming about a better future is a fruitless folly. Realising that another war is coming George knows he is going to find himself living in a humourless, grey country with uniformed revolutionary types hanging about on every street corner.

When he wins seventeen quid on the horses, George keeps the news to himself. Usually he spends illicit cash on booze and tarts, but recently George has found himself reminiscing about his village childhood spent fishing and reading. Those remote days seem golden, far preferable to the suburban drudgery George is now committed to for the rest of his days. The seventeen pounds will fund a return trip to his birthplace, as George has unfinished business there: in a dappled pond hidden by the shadow of trees there may still lurk a pike of legendary dimensions that no-one was ever able to land. Will George recapture the magic of his youth or discover that you really can't go home again?

Full of intimate descriptive writing and plain yet wistful nostalgia, ***Coming Up For Air*** gets our vote as Orwell's finest novel after his masterworks ***Animal Farm*** and ***Nineteen Eighty-Four***. Arguably the first volume of a thematic trilogy exploring the dangers of Totalitarianism to be followed by the books mentioned above (Orwell actually intended to write a family saga that would culminate in the future world of Big Brother), the book's depiction of the protagonists' days as a grocer's son in Edwardian England recalls the social novels and background of H.G. Wells, while critiquing the forces that created the emergent shabby-genteel lower middle classes of the 1930s. Orwell's little-discussed deep love of nature shines through keenly in this touching meditation on boyhood and the horrors of aging, revealing the manfully gentle side of one of the twentieth century's most popular literary authors.

See also: *100 Must-Read Classic Novels*

Read on

Keep The Aspidistra Flying; *The Lion and the Unicorn: Socialism and the English Genius* (NF); *Essays* (NF)

Patrick Hamilton, *The Gorse Trilogy*; Julian McClaren-Ross, *Of Love and Hunger*

CHUCK PALAHNIUK (b 1962) USA

FIGHT CLUB (1996)

Fight Club opens like a **››** J.G. Ballard nightmare; a man with a gun barrel jammed into his mouth waits atop the world's tallest skyscraper as it begins to explode and collapse beneath him.

Rewind to the insomniac narrator seeking a reassuring hopelessness by attending support groups for sufferers of various afflictions. A young woman, Marla, begins to turn up at the same meetings and they identify each other for the frauds they are. And then there is Tyler, a cinema projectionist who splices single frames of genitalia into family films. It is Tyler who the insomniac calls when his apartment gets blown up and together they discover that there is nothing more therapeutic than beating the bejesus out of one another.

In this instant, Fight Club is spawned: a secretive conclave of everyday men who find a release valve in the religion of their fists. One on one, battering your opponent into submission or unconsciousness, then returning to work, never discussing your violent pastime even with fellow members. These are fatherless men and Fight Club is their surrogate masculine influence, the route to their tethered primal selves. Alongside their ever-expanding bare knuckle empire, Tyler (who is sleeping with Marla, much to the narrator's chagrin) and his protégé make soap, which is a couple of simple processes short of manufacturing dynamite, and soon the club members become embroiled in seamier and more nefarious activities as the novel builds to a remarkable climax.

Palahniuk hits hard but he can also do funny. *Fight Club* (his first published novel) is a smart but disquieting book, an illicit, filthy pleasure. The author spent time prior to his writing career working with the homeless and incurably sick, as well as being a journalist. His overt attempts to disturb readers and publishers have led to manuscript rejection, alleged instances of fainting, and of course a huge fanbase.

Film version: *Fight Club* (1999)

Read on

Survivor; *Choke*; *Haunted*

Anthony Burgess, *A Clockwork Orange*; ›› Bret Easton Ellis, *Lunar Park*

TONY PARSONS (b. 1955) UK

STORIES WE COULD TELL (2005)

London, 16 August 1977: Elvis dies, Buzzcocks sign to United Artists. Terry, Leon and Ray are three young journalists who write for a music paper. Although the *sturm und drang* of Punk rages around him, Ray remains fixated on the Fab Four. Leon is politically committed, concerned about the rise of the National Front and sickened by the jingoism of the Silver Jubilee. Terry has just returned from Berlin, where he has been hanging out with Dag Wood, legendary outsider rock star, the only performer to be bottled offstage at Woodstock for being a decade ahead of his time.

In one night, the lives of the three young men will be altered irrevocably. Terry has the most to lose, as he senses Dag Wood moving on his independently-minded girlfriend. Will Terry's idol betray him by stealing the love of his life? These problems are complicated by the realities of avoiding clashes with Teddy Boys and the ***Clockwork Orange***-style yobs known as the Dagenham Dogs, rabid followers of the Sewer Rats, a group whose head-crushing music contrasts thrillingly with their championing of Mao and the MC5.

Employing opaquely-veiled autobiography and composite portraits of actual rockers and journos, ***Stories We Could Tell*** is splendid diversion of the first order, combining dramatic plotting, touching characterisation in good old-fashioned storytelling. Although it was undoubtedly Parson's main intention to comment upon growing up, the true genius of the book lies in its vividly imagined alternative London. Although this author suggests that the book might owe some debt to Todd Haynes' film ***Velvet Goldmine*** in this respect, Parsons cleverly wrong-foots the reader – just when you think you know who Wood or the Sewer Rats are, their closest real-life equivalents are mentioned in the text.

Parsons joined the ***NME*** alongside future wife Julie Burchill. For those of us who found it hard to reconcile the Punk scribe of our youth with the 'Dad Lit' author of bestselling reflections on family life that have strummed a chord with so many men, ***Stories We Could Tell*** reassures us that the rock and roll dreams of our youth were as sweet and significant in making us what we are as we always knew they were.

Read on

The Kids; *Man and Boy*

The facts behind *Stories We Could Tell* (all NF): David Buckley, ***No Mercy: The Authorised and Uncensored Biography of The Stranglers***; Paul Gorman, ***In Their Own Write: Adventures in the Music Press***; Nick Kent, ***The Dark Stuff***; Iggy Pop (with Anne Wehrer), ***I Need More***; John Savage, ***England's Dreaming***

DAVID PEACE (b. 1967) UK

THE DAMNED UNITED (2006)

In 1962, injury brought a premature end to Brian Clough's football playing days. We catch up with him twelve years later, when he has just been appointed manager of a team he loathes, the notoriously poorly disciplined Leeds United. This fictional, first person narrative embraces Clough's bitterness, cussedness and abrasiveness as he recalls earlier forays into management and sets about building a future in the unlikeliest of environments.

The Damned United is the story of Clough's forty-four day tenure at an institution that under Don Revie was already hugely successful, so this is no rags to riches tale. Clough desires to put his own stamp on the team, cutting out the cheating whilst upholding a winning tradition. His honest, self-confident approach worked at Hartlepool and Derby but the Leeds boys hate him for what he has said about them in the past and for the way he treats them now, and the paranoia that has always lurked beneath his assured façade soon rears up. Determined to exorcise the spirit of Revie, Clough burns desks and plots the casting adrift of international players to form a squad he can call his own. At times Clough's stream of consciousness is a litany of hatefulness, the bilious chant of one who believes the whole world is against him, but this is the story of a man with the talent and fibre to back up his convictions, however many enemies he makes along the way. Spectacular failure will eventually lead to great success, albeit with a less stubborn, more malleable club than 'dirty' Leeds.

This is a very daring piece of work, not least because of the opinionated narrator's criticisms of the many real life figures in the novel (the rugged pairing of Billy Bremner and Norman Hunter to name but two), but also because it is a sports novel that aspires to and succeeds as literature. David Peace was born in Yorkshire and came to prominence with a quartet of novels set at the time of the Yorkshire Ripper murders. He now lives in Japan, the setting for his most recent book, *Tokyo Year Zero*.

TV series: *The Damned United* (in production 2008)

Read on

The Red Riding Quartet; *GB84*

Ken Bray, ***How To Score: The Science of the Beautiful Game*** **(NF)**; Tom Bower, ***Broken Dreams*** **(NF)**; Hunter Davies, ***The Glory Game*** **(NF)**; Duncan Hamilton, ***Provided You Don't Kiss Me*** **(NF)**

DONN PEARCE (b. 1928) USA

COOL HAND LUKE (1965)

More men than women go to prison so consequently the definitive texts of jailhouse writing are by men. While the fundamental pains of confinement are the same everywhere, the devil is in the detail. One of the harshest penal regimes of recent times was the chain gang. Donn Pearce used his own experience of working the roads five days a week beneath the eyes of armed guards and a pitiless blazing sun as the guts of a novel.

Lloyd Jackson is a war hero and hellraiser, a disarming free spirit with an authority problem. After arriving at the rural correctional facility that houses the road gangs of 1950s Florida, Jackson establishes himself as a respected character amongst other felons. Although a sharp poker-player, it is his prodigious appetite that clinches his status: championed by Dragline, the bullish con whose loquacity dominates the gang, Jackson wagers that he can eat fifty eggs at one sitting. Jackson's ebullience raises the hackles of the bosses, who set out to break the banjo-playing, wisecracking dude known to his peers as Cool Hand Luke. Jackson has nerve and balls, but the bastards are determined to grind him down at any cost. Unlike the backstabbing delinquents in captivity narratives such as ›› Edward Bunker's ferocious *The Animal Factory*, the chain gang enjoy cordial relationships, but even Jackson's emboldening affect can be stilled by the severity of the punishment meted out to the cheeky malefactor.

Pearce was a sailor, safecracker and private detective. He also wrote the screenplay of the memorable film of his first novel, a masterly adaptation that possess all the lucid cadences of the book's composed, humble prose. Never judgemental, Pearce nevertheless demands we ask ourselves if it is better to be patient and acquiesce or rail against the liberties taken by those who enforce the law. *Cool Hand Luke* is a forlorn, stately elegy for all who have been horribly abused in the name of justice and one of the finest books produced by a former convict.

Film version: *Coolhand Luke* (1967)

Read on

Clink lit: Jimmy Boyle, *A Sense of Freedom* (NF); Malcolm Braly, *On The Yard*; ›› Edward Bunker, *The Animal Factory*; George Jackson, *Soledad Brother* (NF); ›› Jack London, *The Star Rover*

HARRY PEARSON (b. 1961) UK

ACHTUNG SCHWEINEHUND! (2007) (NF)

When Harry Pearson and his mates start a board games night as a response to their wives' attendance of a reading group, they wonder if any of their fellow forty-somethings are sad enough to attend. To their surprise, membership is quickly over-subscribed and Harry finds himself accosted in the street by strangers eager to join in the childish yet satisfying fun.

Like the majority of men born before the late seventies, Pearson grew up in a Britain whose collective consciousness was still dominated by the Second World War. With plenty of relatives who took part in the conflict or suffered its privations, Pearson's childhood dreams of heroism, adventure and victory are sublimated into playing soldiers, reading *Commando* comics and constructing Airfix kits. As Pearson matures he remains faithful to his boyhood vision of combat glory and as an adult he becomes a serious wargamer and collector of lead soldiers.

Achtung Schweinehund! is a comical and poignant account of what it was like to grow up brandishing a toy submachine pistol and giving an extravagant impression of an agonising, Peckinpah-style demise in a hail of imaginary dum-dum bullets, surrounded by Action Men while *Colditz* was showing on the telly. Pearson's vividly detailed reminiscences will have you chuckling away, prompting memories of your own days as a fearless warrior of the local waste ground to return with a vengeance.

Despite the inevitable descent into nerdity such a book guarantees, there are few men who will be unable to relate to Pearson's paen to the realms of collecting and shed-based hobbies. Packed with amusing anecdotes about eccentric individuals whose passion for their pastime results in surfeits of model Hitite chariots crammed into bottom drawers, ***Achtung Schweinehund!*** will ring a bell with anyone who has ever run up a credit card bill on boy's stuff when they should have been installing a new boiler instead.

Read on

A Man About a Dog

James Delingpole, ***Coward on the Beach***; Sven Hassell, ***Blitzfreeze***; Steve Holland (ed.), ***Death or Glory*** (***Battle Picture Library*** anthology); George Low (ed.), ***Commando: The Dirty Dozen*** (***Commando*** comic anthology)

CHRISTOPHER PRIEST (b. 1943) UK

THE SEPARATION (2002)

At a bookshop signing to promote his latest hardcover, Stuart Grattan meets the daughter of J.L. Sawyer, an obscure wartime figure mentioned in Churchill's memoirs. Following Grattan's research into Sawyer – paradoxically described as a conscientious objector and RAF bomber pilot – through letters, diaries and official sources, we realise the historian lives in a world where conflict between Germany and Britain ended peacefully in 1941.

Flashback to 1936: identical twins Jack and Joe Sawyer win rowing bronze at the Berlin Olympics and are introduced to arrogant Nazi Rudolph Hess. Sibling rivalry arising both from varying ideologies and personal feelings begins to divide the brothers when Joe smuggles a Jewish girl both twins love out of Germany. When war breaks out, RAF hero Jack is seconded to Churchill's staff to study Hess, who has flown to Scotland to strike a peace deal. Confusion around J.L. Sawyer's identity develops while Jack's twin status allows him revelatory insights into the personas of Hitler and Hess. Jack's discoveries are only the initial layers of the multiple separations that will sunder not only Jack and Joe (who is bitterly opposed to war) but the future path of history itself. Sometimes men really do live in worlds of their own.

Blending the SF 'alternate history' motif with actual events, sieving both through narrators of questionable reliability, Priest's measured style and subtle narrative obfuscations mesh seamlessly, encouraging us to consider the differences between subjective truth and objective facts. No matter how vigilant the reader, Priest will confound him, laying intentional blanks and ambiguities into his stories that will spur you into re-reading. Readers luxuriating in enigmatic narratives will be besotted by Priest's defiance of firm notions of reality and his perfectly imperfect, shattering climaxes. The doppelganger is a recurrent Priestian theme (as in recently filmed novel *The Prestige*) and in *The Separation*, numerous men will also recognise the uncomfortable tension of enmity and love that characterises sibling relationships.

Often described as an SF writer who turned away from the genre, another view is that Priest's continual inventiveness and matchless blurring of boundaries between literary gamesmanship, metaphysical thriller and historical novel has simply enriched the scope of SF, his apparently cross-genre titles recently reaching a larger, deserved readership thanks to the aforementioned film. We have no doubt that Priest (a father of twins) is comfortable with the difficulty in pigeonholing his works, understanding that some readers prefer being challenged instead of patronised.

See also: *100 Must-Read Science Fiction Novels*

Read on

Fugue For a Darkening Island; *The Extremes*

Alternative histories: Robert Cowley, ***What If?*** (NF); ›› Len Deighton, *SS-GB*; Philip K. Dick, ***The Man in the High Castle***; ›› Robert Harris, *Fatherland*

JOHN RECHY (b. 1934) USA

CITY OF NIGHT (1963)

One of the most splendid novels ever to emerge from American counterculture has remained a forgotten book in Britain for too long. Exploring the need to express one's personal freedom in a manner more focused than Kerouac's ***On The Road***, with an outlaw fearlessness that rivals that of ›› William S. Burroughs, John Rechy's astonishing semi-autobiographical *City Of Night* demands attention from all mature readers.

Why has a novel of such high calibre been so neglected? The answer may lie in its subject matter. While drugs, fast cars and petty criminality might seem romantic to many readers with a streak of rebelliousness, homosexual prostitution is a true underground activity few would feel comfortable identifying with. John Rechy once embraced this occupation.

Johnny Rio is a muscular young Texan feeling the need to escape his painful past. Embracing the liberation drifting brings, he sets out to discover the underbelly of America. From New York to Chicago, from New Orleans to San Francisco, Johnny hustles, selling his body non-reciprocally to gay men of many persuasions – aging fairies, leather fetishists, sadomasochists and flamboyant, cross-dressed queens. Johnny's sexual odyssey into the arenas of neon, police brutality and professional competitiveness from other 'youngmen', allow him to both lose and find his identity. Uncertain of the question he is asking himself, Johnny uncompromisingly seeks the answer by immersing himself in the degradation and euphoria of amoral pandemonium that is 1960s America.

Remote yet impassioned, ***City of Night*** is a work of extraordinary power and commitment. Indicating man's knack for distancing his subjectivity from extreme situations while involving himself utterly, this supremely gifted writer adeptly expresses the vehemence of male sexual desire and the welcome relief of physical and psychic release. No matter that the protagonists of the book are homosexual, few men would be unimpressed by Rechy's courage, honesty and coolness of tone. Too often pigeonholed as merely a 'Gay Classic', this existential masterwork deserves to be read by everyone wishing to understand what it really means to be an outsider.

Sequel: *Numbers*

Read on

Rushes; *The Sexual Outlaw* (NF)

Jake Arnott, ***Johnny Come Home***; Jean Genet, ***The Thief's Journal***; Bertie Marshall, ***Berlin Bromley*** (NF)

LUKE RHINEHART (aka GEORGE COCKCROFT)

(b. 1932) USA

THE DICE MAN (1971)

Doctor Rhinehart is a rather passive psychiatrist, who has been pacified in domestic life by an adherence to Zen, much to the infuriation of his wife. At the end of an evening of cards and futile philosophising, Rhinehart picks up a dice in a fit of nihilistic gloom and decides that he will rape his colleague's wife if he rolls a one. The assault appears to pass off without consequence, owing to Arlene's happy reciprocation, and in any case he conveniently blames fate and his solemn promise to obey the dice.

Widening the possibilities of chance governing decisions, he allows the dice to become his master and he shocks his patients with random and often extreme remedies. Inexorably, the dice fetish grows to an overwhelming compulsion. Numbers dictate what he reads and whom he speaks to or seduces, and the effects become more significant as his very being is transformed to the point that what he fears most is free will. As the comical yet serious (and in many instances shocking) narrative progresses, Rhinehart establishes the much derided but widely adopted dice therapy and wonders to himself whether the perfectly 'Random Man' can ever exist.

The legacy of ***The Dice Man*** is extensive (in some ways mirroring the fictional cult following which emerges during the novel) and there are references in songs, advertisements, plays and even travel programmes. Between 1998 and 2000, ***Loaded*** magazine ran an experiment on living by the dice and it is believed that Cockcroft tried it out himself when working as a university lecturer before conceiving the idea of the novel.

See also: *100 Must-Read Life-Changing Books*

Sequels: *The Search for the Dice Man*; *The Book of the Die*

Read on

Jack Black, ***You Can't Win*** (NF); David Mamet, ***Glengarry Glen Ross*** (drama); Walter Tevis, ***The Queen's Gambit***

GRAHAM ROBB (b. 1958) UK

RIMBAUD (2000) (NF)

Arthur Rimbaud (1854–91) has long been a legend. No other figure could claim to have inspired as many rebels in the last century or more, for Rimbaud's effect on modern culture is all-encompassing, often reaching us indirectly via other artists touched by his seminal works. His famous axiom that the poet should make himself a seer by systematically deranging his senses reached millions when rock stars Jim Morrison, Richard Hell and Patti Smith all embraced Rimbaud's philosophy.

Rimbaud was a French Catholic of provincial origins who relocated to Paris in his late teens. The modest amount of striking poetry and incendiary prose his reputation resides upon was all written by the time he was twenty. The key figure of the Symbolist movement, spiky of hair and manner, Rimbaud famously had an affair with Paul Verlaine, another poet with a penchant for absinthe. One day the pair had a quarrel that led to Rimbaud being shot in the hand and the truth behind what actually happened remains unknowable. After giving up poetry, Rimbaud located to Africa. Legend has it that he became a gun-runner, never taking up the pen again, unaware what effect his tiny literary oeuvre would have. ***Rimbaud*** dives deep into the secrets of the poet's life to reveal a man whose substantial myth is actually less astonishing than the more fascinating truth. As an explorer of interior and exterior territories, Rimbaud is unmasked as a far more significant figure than even his most ardent admirers suspected.

Graham Robb is one of the finest literary biographers working in the world today. A recipient of a number of prestigious awards, Robb is no mere artisan. ***Rimbaud*** is his magnum opus, proving that biography, like the novel, can legitimately be regarded as art. ***Rimbaud***'s pioneering odyssey through both visionary poetry and remote foreign places represents the cardinal quest for self-discovery that has obsessed modern man. Discovering the amazing life of this astounding icon is a trip we believe all men should take and Graham Robb is the finest guide a reader could wish for.

Read on

The Discovery of France (NF)

Crazed visionaries: Phil Baker (ed.), *The Dedalus Book of Absinthe*; **››** William S. Burroughs, *The Place of Dead Roads*; Comte De Lautreamont, ***Maldoror***; Arthur Rimbaud, ***A Season In Hell***

PHILIP ROTH (b. 1933) USA

PORTNOY'S COMPLAINT (1969)

Alex Portnoy is a smart, well-behaved Jewish boy who is unsure why his busybody mother is so inclined to torment and threaten him (often by brandishing a bread knife) whilst simultaneously suffocating him with self-centred love. Growing up to be a champion masturbator and serial monogamist with an aversion to marital commitment, Alex puts his obsession with playing with his prong anywhere and everywhere down to his mother's inestimably incorrect method of teaching him to urinate standing up. Indeed, this hideous yet brilliantly realised caricature of overbearing affection does seem to blame for Portnoy's many imbalances of character.

Projecting his insatiable lust onto others (both secretively and openly) proves to be the bane of Alex's life, as dismal initiations and staged threesomes fail to come off as hoped. His fanatical sexuality dents and warps his grand moral framework, leaving him perennially ashamed, and this is the essence of the affliction that Roth dubs 'Portnoy's Complaint'.

Scathingly critical of the insular bigotry of the older generation (whose pride in their Jewish heritage and distrust of the goyim blinker them beyond belief), pornographic for its time, Roth's first novel is imbued with stunning wit and his commentaries on existence are frequently hilarious if at times unpalatable. Had Woody Allen pursued a literary career, this novel might have been the result.

Roth's characters are often highly sexed and, in *The Breast*, a man is actually transformed into the titular object. But it was the author's harsh criticism of Jewish traditionalists in which elicited most alarm – being kosher himself certainly did not immunise him to the wrath of certain sectors of his community, although he has always been dedicated to examining Jewish identity within American society with gravity as well as humour. Consequently, Roth has long been considered one of the most important US novelists of the last half-century.

Read on

My Life As A Man; *Sabbath's Theatre*; *The Human Stain*
David Sedaris, ***Dress Your Family in Corduroy and Denim***; Kurt Vonnegut, ***Breakfast of Champions***

LEOPOLD VON SACHER-MASOCH

(1836–95) Poland

VENUS IN FURS (1870)

It's not uncommon for a term derived from an author's name to enter the language, but it is unusual when such a word becomes so commonplace that its root is largely forgotten. The word masochism (often coupled with the prefix Sado, after the Marquis de Sade) was coined by psychiatrist Krafft-Ebing and owes its existence solely to the author of ***Venus in Furs***.

Immortalised in the classic Velvet Underground song, the book questions whether men and women can ever be true companions while inequality between the sexes remains by telling the story of Severin, a man inebriated by (yet fearful of) a picture of Venus draped in furs. When he meets Wanda, the embodiment of his inanimate goddess, Severin has to possess her, but she is not one to be the chattel of a single lover. Severin agrees instead to be her slave, hoping to win Wanda by playing the part to her satisfaction, begging to be her thrall. With a whip in her hand, Wanda proves by far the more adept performer. The emotional contortions Severin endures in Wanda's company are excruciating, their games torturous. Several deft reversals occur which threaten to turn the narrative on its head and von Sacher-Masoch's staggering (but nowadays criminally neglected) literary skill is evident in what is a near-perfect piece of writing. Although only some men will find the book sexy, all should read it.

Just as ›› George Cockcroft (Luke Rhinehart) adhered for a time to the dice-destiny of his novels, Von Sacher-Masoch lived out the self-flagellating fantasies of his own books in various relationships. A large proportion of the novel is taken directly from his own experience but he manages also to hold up a mirror to the rest of us men, asking how readily we would renounce our masculine authority once our knees have weakened in appreciation of a woman's allure.

Read on

Wanda von Sacher-Masoch, ***The Confessions of Wanda Von Sacher-Masoch*** (NF); The Marquis de Sade, ***120 Days of Sodom***; ›› Henry Miller, ***Opus Pistorum*** (aka ***Under The Roofs of Paris***); ›› Alexander Trocchi, ***White Thighs***; Herman Ungar, ***The Maimed***

J.D. SALINGER (b. 1919) USA

THE CATCHER IN THE RYE (1945)

The Catcher in the Rye is written in a colloquial style that at first appears simplistic – childish even – but closer inspection reveals Salinger as a masterful observer of human nature. When anti-hero Holden Caulfield, about to be expelled from yet another school, remarks that people always think something is all true he nails the perennial problem of characterisation. He acts young for his age but sometimes he doesn't. It is true of just about any personality trait in anybody you care to think of, and it is particularly relevant to the modern male setting out on adult life.

As he kills time, phoning girls and chatting to an unreceptive prostitute whilst waiting for his parents to learn of his latest academic failure, Holden passes repetitive judgement on whatever comes his way, but we soon recognise that he has a certain perceptiveness – a genuine, average kid's understanding of how the world works. For example, he sees right through thespians essentially worshipped for overacting (Olivier gets a memorable working over). Because Salinger does not portray Caulfield as a precocious know-it-all, we are all the more inclined to listen to what this blueprint for angst-ridden youth has to say.

Salinger is rather harder to pin down than his most famous creation. A recluse who once lost a girlfriend to Charlie Chaplin, his family life was tumultuous: for example, his wife's plot to murder their sick baby daughter then commit suicide did not – thankfully – come to fruition. At one time wooed by the Scientologists, he is a longstanding acolyte Zen Buddhism. He fought in World War II during which he formed an acquaintance with » Ernest Hemingway.

See also: *100 Must-Read Life-Changing Books*

Read on

Franny and Zooey

Angst-ridden adolescents: Jonathan Safran Foer, ***Everything Is Illuminated***; Siri Hustvedt (wife of ›› Paul Auster), ***What I Loved***; ›› Yukio Mishima, ***The Sailor Who Fell From Grace With The Sea***; D.B.C. Pierre, ***Vernon God Little***; Brady Udall, ***The Miracle Life of Edgar Mint***;

JAMES SALTER (b. 1925) USA

THE HUNTERS (1956)

Cleve Connell is a naturally gifted flyer. Calmly assured, serene almost in his mastery of the new F86 jet fighters that are engaging in dogfights with Russian MIGs over Korea, Cleve is quietly confident that his tour as Flight Leader will allow him to become an ace – a pilot who has downed five enemy planes. To be one of this elite, to win the admiration of his peers is the only cause that matters to him. The thought of the wider glory that comes with military heroism means nothing.

Cleve takes command of his flight, relishing the purity of experience missions over enemy territory brings. Yet his quiet confidence begins to wane as other, less experienced pilots get the lucky breaks that evade Cleve, sometimes claiming kills of questionable provenance. Somehow, when Cleve is airborne, MIGs are nowhere to be seen or appear on the horizon only when fuel limitations force his F86 to return to base. As Cleve's disquiet grows, Pell, a fellow airman with a visible hunger for fame unbecoming of the selflessness the squadron routinely displays, adds red stars to his fuselage as his kills rack up. Soon the unspoken rivalry between the men comes to haunt Cleve's every waking hour. With only one star on his plane and the end of his tour approaching, can Cleve live with the knowledge that he, the better pilot, may never regain the respect of his contemporaries?

Salter himself flew F86s over Korea. A world-class writer whose verbal proficiency is a fine metaphor for the pin-point dexterity of fighter pilots, Salter's radiant prose displays sterling imagination balanced with consummate judgement in selecting words. Instead of filling his book with technospeak, Salter instead takes sheer, unadorned poetry and marries it to mercurial action with a clarity that soars miles above the faux-adrenalin of pulp clichés. Cleve's purity of intention is expressed with telling insight and the reader will never forget the devastating climax of *The Hunters*, a story that reveals much of the truth behind the distinction of war heroism and the complex relationships between competitors.

Read on

Light Years; *Burning The Days* (NF)

Air men: Antoine De Saint-Exupery, ***Southern Mail***; Manfred Von Richthofen, ***Red Baron*** (NF); Derek Robinson, ***A Piece of Cake***

ROBERT FALCON SCOTT (1868–1912) UK

JOURNALS (1912) (NF)

Books about exploration tend to read like sports biographies – accounts of victorious arrivals and of doing something before anyone else. Scott came second to Amundsen in the race for the South Pole in 1910–12, and ultimately lost his life but his journals are so much more than a gamesman's notebook. For one thing, Scott's naturalist enthusiasm and humanitarian sensibilities show through in entries concerning wildlife, geological formations and the welfare of his team (down to the dogs and ponies essential to the expedition, who are clearly valued by Scott as living creatures with names and distinct personalities).

Secondly, there is the very real triumph of crossing the tempestuous ocean and pitiless ice floes as well as the 850-mile journey to safety with resources dwindling which so nearly succeeded. Scott's record is one of men looking into one another's hearts and finding stoicism, bravery and a willingness to sacrifice everything for their comrades, forever praising his men's unity and diligence, implying they held an enormous respect for his captaincy. The motivational and organisational skills required to bring his men through the ultimate battle against nature mark Scott as one of the finest leaders in history, a fact borne out by his many decorations which included the prestigious French Legion of Honour. Reading the last pages of the journals is a heartrending yet strangely uplifting experience, convincing us that he deserved all the respect, all the medals bestowed upon him, and so much more besides. However, there are some who consider Scott to be a self-aggrandising, reckless fool stalking glory at whatever cost (our last two Read on suggestions champion opposite views in this regard).

Scott had ventured to the Antarctic before, including trips with Shackleton and Evans (the latter dying during the final expedition), but it is for his journals that he is most remembered. Without setting out to dramatise what is already supremely epic, the impressions he intermittently sets down read like notes for a novel: who knows what great works Scott might have produced had he survived?

Read on

Alfred Lansing, ***Endurance*** (NF); Sir Ernest Shackleton, ***South*** (NF); Roland Huntford, ***Scott and Amundsen*** (NF); Sir Ranulph Fiennes, ***Captain Scott*** (NF)

READONATHEME: SUPERMAN

Celebrating the inspirational audacity of men of genius and ambiguity

Luis Buñuel, ***My Last Breath*** (NF)
Harlan Ellison, ***Memos From Purgatory*** (NF)
Brian Eno, ***A Year With Swollen Appendices*** (NF)
Albert Hoffman, ***LSD My Problem Child*** (NF)
Jack Kerouac, ***Lonesome Traveller***
T.E. Lawrence (352087A/c Ross), ***The Mint*** (NF)
Fillipo-Tomasso Marinetti, ***Mafarka The Futurist***

» Yukio Mishima, ***Sun and Steel*** (NF)
Friedrich Nietzsche, ***Ecce Homo*** (NF)
Henry David Thoreau, ***Walden/Civil Disobedience*** (NF)

HUBERT SELBY (1928–2004) USA

THE DEMON (1976)

Before ***American Psycho*** and ***Fight Club*** there was ***The Demon***.

Harry White is possessed by overwhelming animal urges. A thrusting young executive, he is a restless sexual predator spending his lunch hours stalking women for carnal conquest. As Harry's career star ascends he experiences the odd wobble when his insatiable lust overcomes his ambition, putting his working future in jeopardy. Marrying the adorable Linda, who touches something in him no other woman has reached, Harry is made vice-president of the firm and the perfect couple purchase a cottage, a fitting home for their baby son. Despite this outward success, Harry's hidden genital gluttony combines with the pressures of work to threaten his sanity. Some kind of devil lurks inside him, eager to overpower its host. Madness beckons Harry, and with its licence to lose control the possibility of violence may cease to be a mere threat.

Experiencing ***The Demon*** is more like succumbing to severe delirium than reading. The reader inhabits Harry's feverish consciousness, assuming the mantle of a man driven by his id, the subconscious dark side of the personality that is usually concealed even from its owner. A searing assault upon the stifling nature of conformity, exposing the hypocrisy behind the genteel image of so many responsible family men, ***The Demon*** also argues powerfully for society to understand the demands of contemporary lifestyles that clash so contrastingly with the fight-or-flight body chemistry we inherited from our ancestors. Aside from his genius at expressing the interior agonies of a man bullied by his own testosterone (making the book an essential read for women wanting to understand their partners), Selby's compassion shines throughout ***The Demon***, just as it did in ***Last Exit To Brooklyn***, his most famous book. The subject of a notorious obscenity case, ***Last Exit*** (despite its brilliance) has unfairly overshadowed Selby's other work. One of America's finest avant-garde writers, some-time heroin addict Selby was ahead of his time and quietly influential, remaining undiscovered by many readers who would worship his bleak yet tender oeuvre. ***The Demon*** is in our view his most underrated book, a masterpiece that deserves the widest possible recognition.

Read on

Requiem For A Dream

Paul Bowles, ***Let it Come Down***; William S. Burroughs Jnr., ***Kentucky Ham***; John Fante, ***Ask The Dust***; Herbert Huncke, ***The Evening Sun Turned Crimson*** (NF)

WILL SELF (b. 1961) UK

THE BOOK OF DAVE (2006)

A bitter taxi driver's letters to his son are found five hundred years hence by the inhabitants of Ham, the only part of the central London not underwater. His misogynistic, racist writings, 'The Book of Dave', become the cornerstone of all English society. Time is divided into tariffs based on the periods of varied taxi fares, the sun is the 'headlight' and the moon a 'fog lamp'. Most importantly, mums and dads are each allotted time to spend with children but are forbidden to live as husband and wife, reflecting Dave's acrimonious break-up with his wife.

Dave produced these sheets of printed metal for the benefit of his son whom he worships but never sees and can never truly relate to. Chapters in Self's novel alternately follow Dave vindictively digging up dirt on his ex's new bloke whilst hankering after his lost boy like so many other fathers who see the law as being weighted in favour of the mother (some of his friends are members of a protest group based on Fathers for Justice), and the simple islanders of the future (the Hamsters) striving to show their worth to the God whose scriptures are all they know. But one resident of Ham is not so accepting of the 'Holy' book's doctrine. Claiming to have found a second, far more tolerant and caring book of Dave's outpourings, Symun anoints himself as the Messiah (the Geezer) and sets about changing the mindset of his small community. After Symun is exiled, his son follows in his footsteps, hoping to discover the truth behind his legacy.

The Book of Dave is a beguiling parody of the way religions germinate and envelop populations. It is also about misguided priorities, of obsession confused with love and is iconoclastic wordmeister and one time heroin addict Will Self at his staggering best.

Read on

My Idea of Fun; *How the Dead Live*

Pierre Boulle, *Planet of the Apes*; Russell Hoban, *Riddley Walker*; Salman Rushdie, *The Moor's Last Sigh*

ROBERT SILVERBERG (b. 1935) USA

THE BOOK OF SKULLS (1972)

What would you do to secure immortality?

In the archives of an ivy-league campus library, intense, insecure Jewish undergraduate Eli Steinfeld stumbles across an ancient, previously undeciphered document. Such is Eli's academic genius that he quickly translates the manuscript. Entitled *The Book of Skulls*, the cryptic work tells of a house where a man might find eternal life. Four initiates must submit to the mysteries of the Skull House, but for a pair of their number to live forever, the others must die.

Believing the location of the Skull House to be in the remoteness of the Arizona desert, Eli convinces his roomies to join his quest. Ned is a would-be writer and homosexual who lusts after Oliver, a strong, silent Kansas farm boy. Timothy, a wealthy cynic who harbours the prejudices that accompany his social status decides to go along just for the ride. As the motley quartet speed across America by car, the narrative weaves sinuously between their four viewpoints, winding tight with tension as the rivalries between the students blossom and wane. Caught between faith and doubt, nagged by fears and hopes, the four prepare themselves for the eruption of personal conflicts that might reward the victors with the ultimate trophy.

A gripping road novel whose needle-sharp tone transcends its fantastic premise, *The Book of Skulls* is one of Silverberg's key books. Rightly famous for his stunning science fiction, Silverberg sold his first novel at the age of seventeen and by the mid-sixties was a millionaire. By that time he had produced numerous, critically acclaimed non-fiction titles (including some on archaeology, no doubt useful when he wrote *The Book of Skulls*) before returning to SF at the end of the sixties, writing a string of breathtaking masterpieces over the next ten years.

Although always packaged as SF, *The Book of Skulls* refuses easy categorisation as you will discover upon finishing the book, so don't be put off by the label. Silverberg's urbane intelligence and fearlessness in dealing with subjects like power, sacrifice and transcendence, matched by his astringent, stainless steel prose is a joy to read. This is an unputdownable introduction to an awesome writer who would be internationally famous had he elected to work in the literary mainstream.

Further information: *100 Must-Read Science Fiction Novels*

Read on

A Time of Changes; *Downward To The Earth*; *Dying Inside*

On the road: James Sallis, *Drive*; Roger Zelazny, *Roadmarks*

DAN SIMMONS (b. 1948) USA

THE SONG OF KALI (1985)

Amongst our collections of modern firsts is a small hardback book that appears somewhat tired. Pages browned due to the cheap paper stock it is printed on, the jacket design is of a four-armed, fanged woman with a severed head depending from one of her hands. For twenty years she has haunted our nights thanks to Dan Simmon's first novel, winner of the World Fantasy Award.

Kali is an Indian goddess of complex character, popularly known as a malign entity of evil, reportedly the patroness of the Thugee cult of religious stranglers. According to Hindu cosmology, we currently live in Kali Yuga, the long dark age. Simmons uses these mythologies to weave a tale of horror rooted in place, reminding us of Stevenson's maxim that 'It is better to travel hopefully than to arrive.'

Robert Luczak is an American poet commissioned to write an article about new verse by M. Dass, a reclusive disciple of Tagore. Luckily, Luczak's wife is of Indian birth and the couple fly to the subcontinent with their baby daughter. From the moment the trio arrive in Calcutta, Luczak is appalled by the squalor, poverty and decay that envelopes the city. Infuriated by the opaque manners and superstitious proclamations of the Indians he suspects are giving him the runaround in his quest to find Dass, Luczak eventually encounters the poet. Repulsed by the latter's Kali-fixated doggerel, Luczak cannot avoid being plunged into the filthy realm of the infernal goddess, who hungers for the sacrifice of a naïve westerner.

Simmons' story is a relentless hymn of the hatred Luczak bears toward Calcutta, conjuring in its evocative prose a miasmic vision of a city as horribly disfigured as the paper of my first edition copy. Although only two pages of the book contain arguably supernatural events, *The Song of Kali* is a superior exercise in terror that fathers in particular will find petrifying. Comfortable writing fiction of all varieties, Simmons is best known for the international bestsellers *The Hyperion Cantos*, an SF tetralogy.

Read on

Carrion Comfort; *The Terror*

William Peter Blatty, *The Exorcist*; T.E.D. Klein, *The Ceremonies*; Joe Roberts, *Abdul's Taxi to Khaligat: A Celebration of Calcutta* (NF, a travel book that presents a fully rounded view of the city, making an excellent foil for Simmons' novel)

JOE SIMPSON (b. 1960) UK

TOUCHING THE VOID (1988) (NF)

Scorning preamble and flowery asides, Simpson's urgent account of the first successful climb of Siula Grande in the Peruvian Andes identifies him as a true adventurer with a staggering story to tell, instead of a writer setting out to accomplish something worth writing about. Fixations with reaching the unreachable are common amongst explorers, but what sets this book apart is the stark narrative of what happens after Simpson and Simon Yates achieve their goal.

Whilst negotiating the treacherous, icy descent, Simpson falls and shatters his tibia. Accepted mountaineering practice is to abandon the stricken team member if this gives the healthy climber the best chance of survival, but Yates attempts to abseil down with his incapacitated friend. Progressing agonisingly, but steadily, Simpson suddenly plummets into darkness. Yates is left straining against his companion's weight whilst perched precariously on a makeshift snow seat which is disintegrating minute by minute. Before long, Yates realises he has to make a dreadful choice – sever the rope or be dragged into the abyss.

Simpson's recollections of his miraculous return from the brink of death are heart-thumping. The writing is spare – raw even – and Simpson is unapologetic in not stopping to explain terminology which may pass over the heads of the uninitiated. This stripped down immediacy is ideal as we hear every crumbling rock face, every cracking bone of the ill-fated expedition.

The intrepid Simpson continued to climb, face adversity and also, tragically, to lose friends. In later books he describes the mental toll such experiences have taken on him and how they eventually led to his retiring from such perilous pursuits. As a grim, unadorned portrait of almost reckless bravery, Simpson's works are unmissable.

Film version: *Touching the Void* (2003)

Read on

This Game of Ghosts (NF); *The Beckoning Silence* (NF)

Frances Ashcroft, *Life at the Extremes* (NF); Heinrich Harrer, *The White Spider* (NF); Tom Patey, *One Man's Mountains* (NF)

ICEBERG SLIM aka ROBERT BECK (1918–92) USA

PIMP (1967) (NF)

First memories are so often formative ones, and the image of three-year-old Robert Beck forced to perform a sexual act upon his babysitter is quite an introduction to the life of Chicago's finest pimp. His mama – a naïve country girl – ditches his beloved stepfather, taking up with a slick shyster, and Beck pays for her grave error with three years of abuse at her new lover's hands. But he forgives her for the sins that transform him from a college kid with an IQ of 175 into a crook.

As a fledgling hoodlum, Iceberg rents out his girlfriend, dresses as a whore to assist his hustler-mentor's scams and is framed for a burglary. In and out of the slammer, he prepares himself for his unusual calling and dreams of being a master pimp. Apparently the key to successful pimping involves always having a ready retort to keep your ladies under your thumb and Iceberg's street argot is as quick and witty on paper as it indubitably was during his distinguished career (be prepared for regular visits to the glossary at the back of the book though). Fortunately, Iceberg has not been over-edited, so although his staccato sentences are sometimes stilted, they are always authentic.

By the 1940s, Iceberg is wise to the cons attempted upon him and begins to take command of his patch. The action is raw and downright nasty – it is not just harsh words he lays on wayward prostitutes – and *Pimp* is a window onto a world readers may reject as despicably misogynistic, but it was and remains a reality for numerous black men. The context is crucial: black people were regularly barred from most legitimate lucrative professions and crime was often their only route to prosperity.

It was not until the early sixties that Slim retired from his illicit trade and went straight, writing ***Pimp*** as a cautionary tale. His honesty and insight into a seedy underworld earned him immense respect whilst not exactly dissuading his rapping followers from wanting to emulate him, at least in their imaginations.

Read on

The Naked Soul of Iceberg Slim (NF); *Long White Con* (NF)
Alfred Gholson, ***The Pimp's Bible*** (NF); Sanyika Shakur, ***Monster*** (NF); Terrell Wright, *Home of the Body Bags* (NF)

RICHARD STARK aka DONALD E. WESTLAKE

(b. 1933) USA

SLAYGROUND (1969)

Parker is unemotional, always professional, economical with words, adaptable and inventive. He moves unpredictably and is swift as quicksilver. Tall, broad, impassive and harder than iron, he is the consummate heist expert. Only two things can wrongfoot Parker – working with amateurs and blind bad luck.

After an armoured car knockover is blown by a nervous driver who crashes the getaway vehicle in his haste, Parker is forced to abandon his partner-in-crime Grofield as the sound of sirens closes in. Having grabbed the take, but desperate for cover from the police, Parker scales the fence of Funland, an amusement park shut down for the winter.

Unknown to the perfectionist thief, two cops receiving their regular payoff from a couple of local mobsters have observed Parker's escape from the crash. Connecting the robbery with the events they have witnessed, the quartet decide to cash in. But when they venture into Parker's dark, freezing hideout, they find themselves up against a ruthless, resourceful operator who intends to both retain his prize and survive the coming night no matter how overwhelming the odds against him appear.

Slayground is possibly the greatest piece of sustained action writing ever committed to print. In prose as clear as a recently squeegeed windowpane, Stark lives up to his name as he thrillingly allows the reader to watch fiction's ultimate antihero endure the tightest of corners in his characteristically workmanlike style. Overall, reading the book is such a visual experience that one might as well be watching a film (tragically, the screen adaptation of this excellent crime novel discards virtually all the detail of the book, replacing it with grossly inferior material).

Preaching the gospel that the coolly efficient are most likely to succeed, Richard Stark's twenty-three Parker novels are the beatitudes for existentialists. Although the character's debut (in *The Hunter* aka *Point Blank*) presented him with a conventional motivation, the unique drive of the series soon establishes itself as Parker's sole spur is revealed as cold, hard cash and nothing more. Truly amoral, Parker simply does what is necessary, killing only when the situation demands it.

Donald E. Westlake, author of over one hundred books, is one of America's most feted crime novelists and screenwriters. As Westlake he usually writes comic mysteries, but his most fervent addicts worship his sparse, taut Richard Stark persona.

Film version: *Slayground* (1983)

Sequel: *The Blackbird* (follows the fate of Parker's light-hearted partner Alan Grofield in the aftermath of the crash)

Read on

Writing as Tucker Coe (one of Westlake's many pseudonyms): ***Kinds of Love Kinds of Death***

As Donald E. Westlake: ***361***; ***Sacred Monster***

›› Dan Simmons, ***Hard Case***

The Parker & Grofield Novels: this complete list is in order of internal chronology and incorporates the Grofield novels, which are marked with an asterisk. Note that ***Child Heist*** only features Parker briefly.

The Hunter (aka *Point Blank*); *The Man With The Getaway Face* (aka *The Steel Hit*); *The Outfit*; *The Mourner*; *The Score* (aka *Killtown*); *The Jugger*; *The Split* (aka *The Seventh*); *The Handle* (aka *Run Lethal*); *The Rare Coin Score*; *The Damsel**; *The Green Eagle Score*; *The Dame**; *The Black Ice Score*; *The Sour Lemon Score*; *Deadly Edge*; *The Black Bird**; *Slayground*; *Lemons Never Lie**; *Plunder Squad*; *Butcher's Moon*; *Child Heist* (aka *Jimmy The Kid*); *Comeback*; *Backflash*; *Flashfire*; *Firebreak*; *Breakout*; *Nobody Runs Forever*; *Ask The Parrot*

DANNY SUGERMAN (1955–2005) USA

WONDERLAND AVENUE (1989) (NF)

A wild child with a knack for upsetting authority figures, the arguably spoilt and undeniably hyperactive Danny Sugerman is regularly grounded for bad behaviour. But when he blows up the high school toilets, he knows he'll have to knuckle down to his studies.

Despite the material privileges that accompany a Beverly Hills address, Danny copes with the tribulations of residing with a stepfather he despises by luxuriating in the sweet, dirty sounds of rock and roll. Yet while few teenagers achieve their ambition of meeting their musical idols, Danny's dreams come true when he is employed by The Doors to answer their fan mail. Still at school, Danny finds himself hanging out with notorious singer and poet Jim Morrison, chugging brews alongside the leather-trousered Adonis. When Morrison dies at the age of 27, Danny is devastated – what is he going to do with his life now?

Two years later Danny's career as a music journalist is eclipsed by his move into rock entrepreneurship. Managing the affairs of ex-Doors keyboardist Ray Manzarek, Danny acquires a luscious jailbait girlfriend, a house in Laurel Canyon (home of rich hippy songwriters and Alice Cooper) and a plan for world domination, hooking mellow Manzarek up with self-destructive proto-punk vocalist Iggy Pop. As Pop descends maniacally onto the Sunset Strip, haunting glam rock venue the English Disco and savouring the delights of underage groupies, Danny doesn't realise there is a problem: both manager and singer have unfeasibly elephantine drug habits that even their excessive egos will find hard to beat.

Wonderland Avenue is as hilarious as it harrowing, unashamedly depicting irresponsible, self-indulgent antics enacted in a continuous chemical haze. Although most of us would prefer to enjoy a long life, ***Wonderland Avenue*** nevertheless appeals to the recklessness in all men, prompting us to consider that a short but intense existence has its attractions. Luckily, reading this marvellous book is almost as good as leading such a debauched life and much safer than actually doing it yourself – just have CD copies of *Raw Power* and *Strange Days* handy to play at maximum volume while reading it.

Read on

(With Jerry Hopkins) ***No One Here Gets Out Alive*** (NF)

Joe Ambrose, ***Gimme Danger: The Story of Iggy Pop*** (NF); Barney Hoskins, ***Waiting For The Sun*** (NF); Johnny Rogan, ***Starmakers and Svengalis*** (NF); Craig Kee Strete, ***Burn Down The Night***

READONATHEME: BACK DOOR MAN

Jim Morrison set the standard for literacy and licentiousness amongst rock stars. This reading list reflects his milieu, interests and influences.

Louis-Ferdinand Celine, ***Journey to the End of the Night***
Wallace Fowlie, ***Rimbaud and Jim Morrison*** (NF)
Jack Keruoac, ***Desolation Angels***
Ray Manzarek, ***Light My Fire*** (NF)
Jim Morrison, ***Wilderness: The Lost Writings*** (Poetry, prose)
Friedrich Nietzsche, ***The Birth of Tragedy*** (NF)

» John Rechy, *Body and Soul*
Arthur Rimbaud (Ed. Wallace Fowlie), *Complete Works/Selected Letters*
Sophocles, *The Theban Plays* (Drama)

HUNTER S. THOMPSON (aka ROAUL DUKE)
(1937–2005) USA

FEAR AND LOATHING IN LAS VEGAS (1971) (NF)

Out of their minds on drugs, Hunter Thompson and his boisterous Samoan 'attorney' arrive in Las Vegas in a convertible stacked high with heinous chemicals, their quest to locate and document the American Dream whilst nominally reporting on an off-road auto race called the Mint 400. This is the off-the-cuff, anarchic 'Gonzo journalism' classic for which Thompson is notorious. He is not just part of the story – he *is* the story, and it is a tale told in mock epic style as though by a comprehensible James Joyce on mescaline.

Hapless young hitchhikers; appalled hotel staff; impressionable young girls. The pair's morally lax, factually dodgy but infallibly uproarious encounters are laced with every illicit substance imaginable and decorated with Ralph Steadman's unmistakably noisy and grotesque caricatures, flawlessly complementing Thompson's lurid LSD visions of moray eels and cannibalistic lizards. There is a priceless moment when Thompson realises that the chaotic, dust-cloaked race is actually impossible to cover because you can hardly see a thing apart from the odd careening dune buggy. Then there is the newspaper story of a guy on PCP who tugs his own eyes out ... in the duo's hazy world, it is everyone else who is paranoid: they are merely trying to get the job done. So what if they hit a few pavements and try to drive into a launderette every now and then? Besides, nothing in Thompson's acid-blasted mind seems as warped as everyday Vegas insanity.

Thompson became a sports journalist after a spell in the Air Force, cropping up in ›› Norman Mailer's *The Fight* at ringside. But it is for his subversive approach to reporting that we know and love the man, who committed suicide in 2005, convinced he was past it. Whether living with and being beaten up by Hell's Angels or following the 1972 Presidential campaign, Thompson is a cult hero to men who dream of releasing their safety catches.

Film version: *Fear and Loathing in Las Vegas* (1998)

Read on

The Rum Diary; *The Great Shark Hunt*

Altered states: Aldous Huxley, *The Doors of Perception*; ›› John Rechy, *The Fourth Angel*; ›› Tom Wolfe, *The Electric Kool-Aid Acid Test*

PETER TINNISWOOD (1936–2003) UK

A TOUCH OF DANIEL (1969)

The North, during the industrial boom time of the early sixties. Easy-going factory hand Carter Brandon lives with his verbose mother and earthy father, Les, who is sick to the back teeth with cream crackers, Cheshire cheese and pickled onions for tea every evening. Meanwhile, Carter is facing a similarly conventional matrimonial future with nest-building hairdresser Pat, while being tempted by the casual flirtatiousness of brazen factory bike Linda Preston.

The Brandon ménage soon expands further to incorporate Carter's Auntie Lil and Uncle Mort. Mort is a ribald old geezer whose primary interests are ale, rugby and allotment neglect. Setting an admirably bad example for generations of male Brandons, Mort does nothing to discourage Les and Carter in their preference for spending time in the smoke room of the local, away from the constant nattering of their womenfolk. Mort does more than just talk, however, having just made Auntie Lil pregnant despite her advanced years. After Lil expires after giving birth to baby Daniel, Carter's gentle, fatherly temperament urges him to spend time with the little one, holding imaginary conversations in his head with the infant. Daniel 'responds' silently, berating Carter's soft-heartedness and debating with his carer whether the bondage of wedlock is a better deal than the drunken hollowness of sexual independence.

Warmly affecting as a study of the beery companionship of male bonding, with wonderfully silly characters and hilarious illustrations of the interminable battle of the sexes (consisting of the male urge towards informal irresponsibility versus woman's instinct for home-making and respectability), *A Touch of Daniel* relates situations all men will recognise in their relationships with the fairer sex.

Peter Tinniswood was Britain's Dean of provincial and class comedy, enjoying a successful career as a novelist and TV scriptwriter. The irrepressibly miserable Uncle Mort was played by the iconic Robin Bailey in the BBC series, while the almost-forgotten novels continue to inspire politically incorrect mirth in all who discover them.

TV series: *I Didn't Know You Cared* (1975–79)
Sequels: *I Didn't Know You Cared*; *Except You're A Bird*; *Call it a Canary*
Read on
J.L. Carr, ***How Steeple Sinderby Wanderers Won the F.A. Cup***; John Fortune and John Wells, ***A Melon For Ecstasy***; Tom Sharpe, ***Blott on the Landscape***

ALEXANDER TROCCHI (1925–84) UK

YOUNG ADAM (1954)

Joe lives and works on board a barge that transports coal and other haulage between Glasgow and Edinburgh. Sharing the sparse lifestyle and confined spaces of this miniature wooden world alongside Joe are middle-aged Leslie, his thirty-something wife Ella and their small son Jim. Despite her hardened attitude to existence, Ella is nevertheless attractive to Joe, who is finding the heavy voluptuousness of her flesh increasingly irresistible. Aware that Leslie is impotent, Joe presses his advantage with Ella.

Realising that Leslie will inevitably discover his cuckolded status, Joe merely accepts this eventuality, for he has a more pressing problem he should be worried about: the men have fished the near-naked body of a drowned girl out of the canal. The rest of Joe's ménage does not know that he was once the girl's lover and the Clyde Police are hunting for her murderer, but the bargeman seems unbothered, merely relishing the sensuality of his affair with Ella.

Alex Trocchi was Scotland's answer to the Beat Generation and arguably the spiritual forefather of contemporary Scots writers like Irvine Welsh. A heroin addict for much of his life, Tocchi also lived on barges himself, covering both subjects in his superb autobiographical novel ***Cain's Book***. An archetypal example of the avant-garde 'underground writer' whose species no longer exists in our hyped-up, anything goes media climate, Trocchi's uncluttered, spare prose and existential outlook has long been acclaimed by artists like **»** William Burroughs and Patti Smith.

Trocchi was notorious for putting his wife out on the game and encouraging publishers to pay him advances for books he never wrote, scams designed to bring in cash for drugs. ***Young Adam*** was Trocchi's first non-porn novel, published by Olympia Press, the Parisian house infamous and celebrated for disseminating superior erotica and literary masterpieces by the likes of Nabokov and Henry Miller in the fifties and sixties, which were then too 'obscene' to be issued in the UK. Although all his small oeuvre is worth reading, this British answer to ***The Outsider*** is the ideal place to begin discovering this still little-known literary genius.

Film version: *Young Adam* (2003)

Read on

Helen and Desire; *Thongs*

Allan Campbell and Tim Niel (eds), ***A Life in Pieces: Reflections on Alexander Trocchi*** (a brilliant collection of pieces by and about Trocchi); Alexander McArthur and H. Kingsley Long, ***No Mean City***; Richard Seaver et al (eds.), ***Writers in Revolt*** (NF)

CHARLES WILLEFORD (1919–88) USA

COCKFIGHTER (1972)

Frank Mansfield is as contrary and obstinate as the gamecocks he fights for a living. Principled to the point of strangeness, Frank takes a self-imposed vow of silence after shooting his mouth off about the toughness of one of his chickens immediately before it suffered an ignominious defeat. Almost three years later, Frank still hasn't spoken a word, has seen all his birds killed, losing his trailer and big-breasted teenage girlfriend to a rival cockfighter.

With his fiancée approaching thirty and waiting in their hometown for him to pop the question, Frank realises her patience is wearing thin. But Frank will only be content if he can win the coveted silver medal that has been awarded to only four champions in fifteen years. Playing his guitar to raise a new stake that will allow him to become a contender again, calling in favours, making deals, drinking and womanising, Frank doggedly prepares to win the bloody tournament that will allow him to regain his self-respect and speak to his fellow men once more.

With a focus on the minutiae of the cruel blood sport that will make even the toughest reader flinch, the author paints an arresting picture of Southern life and of a man's desire for achievement that suits his psychological integrity, no matter how absurd it may seem to others. Employing the deft characterisation and realistic dialogue his reputation was built upon, Willeford produced a novel that demands to be admired despite its distasteful subject matter.

Charles Willeford was a soldier, lecturer and one of the finest crime writers who ever lived, authoring the bestselling Hoke Mosely detective capers in the 1980s. But before these Miami-based stories made his name, Willeford produced several peerless noir novels that generally appeared as pulp paperbacks. Most of these are brilliant, incisive studies of the unique motivations of their anti-heroes and as such are essential reading for all men wishing to comprehend the nature of their own individuality.

NB: In the UK, *Cockfighter* is published within *The Charles Willeford Omnibus*.

Film version: *Cockfighter* (1974). Note that the film (which features Willeford himself in a supporting role) has never been shown or sold in the UK – it was refused a certificate as it includes footage of actual cockfights – it has been issued on DVD in the USA.

Read on

Cockfighter Journal (**NF**, Willeford's diary of the making of the film, with a foreword by ›› James Lee Burke); *The High Priest of California*; *The Burnt Orange Heresy*; *Sideswipe*; *Something About A Soldier* (autobiography)

READONATHEME: BAD MAN

French existentialists (such as Camus) were enthusiastic admirers of the noir pulp fiction that came out of America in the fifties. Many of these books were written by authors often described as crime novelists, but are quite different to (and more fascinating than) conventional detective stories in their seedy, romantic focus on amoral outsider figures. French authors like Delacorta and Boris Vian also produced twisted noir inspired by the American greats.

Frederick Brown, *His Name Was Death*
Delacorta (aka Daniel Odier), *Diva*
Steve Fisher, *I Wake Up Screaming*
David Goodis, *Shoot the Piano Player*
Richard Neely, *Shattered*
Jim Thompson, *The Grifters*
Boris Vian, *I Spit On Your Grave*
Charles Williams, *The Hot Spot* aka *Hell Hath No Fury*
Cornel Woolrich, *The Bride Wore Black*

COLIN WILSON (b. 1931) UK

RITUAL IN THE DARK (1960)

Late fifties London: Gerard Sorme has a miniscule private income that allows him to abstain from work while leading a Spartan existence in bedsit land. Sorme has ambitions to become a writer but finds himself irritated by the shallowness of modern life and paralysed into inaction by his struggle to define, experience and maintain the sense of freedom grasped momentarily by artists. Accosted at an exhibition by Austin Nunne, Sorme accepts a drink from this moneyed, indolent homosexual. Wandering Bohemian Soho, the duo booze, feast and debate the elusive meaning of life.

Sorme is drawn into Nunne's circle of acquaintances: Gertrude, the prim spinster who gently attempts to convert Sorme to her religion; Caroline, Gertrude's vivacious niece who is keen to seduce him; and bellicose painter Oliver Glasp, a misanthrope who exudes the moody excesses of a Van Gogh. These and Sorme's fellow lodging house tenants distract the would-be writer from the undercurrent of terror that currently grips the city, for a sex killer with a modus operandi reminiscent of Jack the Ripper has just claimed another victim in the East End. Sorme ponders his philosophical and sexual options, realising that his new friends have greater problems than his own. Questioning his loyalties while using these relationships to answer his questions about existence, he suspects that the serial murderer is more than a shadowy figure in the background of his metaphysical journey.

Usually packaged as a crime novel, Colin Wilson's five-hundred plus page *bildungsroman* is actually more in the tradition of great existential novels such as ***Steppenwolf***, ***Hunger***, ***Crime and***

Punishment and *The Man Without Qualities*. A working class lad from Leicester who left school at sixteen, the author was catapulted to overnight fame as part of the 'Angry Young Man' set with the publication of his first book ***The Outsider*** (1956), a non-fiction study of rebel artists. But while ***The Outsider*** tackles the same issues as ***Ritual in the Dark***, it is the novel that is the superior work, with its evocative Soho atmosphere and dramatically neurotic characters.

Although Wilson has become a cult and has enjoyed massive commercial success – penning over a hundred books in areas as diverse as philosophy, new age, true crime and fiction – his critical reputation has suffered from his tendency towards over-enthusiasm and novelty. Despite this, his rabid fanbase is devoted to his stimulating work, which this commentator believes is often savagely underrated.

Sequels: *Man Without a Shadow* (aka *The Sex Diary of Gerard Sorme* aka *Sex Diary of a Metaphysician*); *The God of the Labyrinth*

Read on

Adrift in Soho; *The Misfits: A Study of Sexual Outsiders* (NF)
Gerald Kersh, *Night and the City*

TOM WOLFE (b. 1931) USA

THE BONFIRE OF THE VANITIES (1987)

Wall Street bond trader Sherman McCoy fancies himself a macho super hero and believes it is his right to have an affair on the basis that he married a (fractionally) older woman who is now more statuesque than sexy. It doesn't augur well when Sherman accidentally dials his home number and asks for his mistress, but matters become inestimably worse when he and the girlfriend find themselves lost in the Bronx driving a flash Merc. They stop at a blocked road and two black men emerge, offering assistance. In his paranoid certainty that they are a pair of stereotypical muggers, Sherman throws a tyre at one and his mistress ends up mowing the other down.

Mistakenly believing that he was legitimately fighting his way out of some kind of jungle, the disdainfully racist McCoy does not report the incident, but community leader Reverend Bacon is determined that the now comatose lad will not be just another statistic – another promising black life wrecked without complaint or consequence. English journalist Farrow picks up on the story after his magazine is accused of racist attitudes and, with the moral bandwagon gaining momentum, Sherman is destined not to walk casually away from his crime, and faces a ruinous fall from his self-appointed pedestal as the truth begins to manifest itself.

Tom Wolfe came to public notice with his journalistic books written in the sixties about the sixties and did not write a novel until ***Bonfire of the Vanities*** was serialised in Rolling Stone magazine. As with his non-fiction, the book came to epitomise the lifestyle and aspirations of men in the decade in which it is set. Wolfe has always received a rancorous reception from the Left, and the novelists John Updike, John Irving and ›› Norman Mailer have also voiced their disapproval of his work, although it is probably fair to say that he wears this unpopularity as a badge of honour.

Film version: *Bonfire of the Vanities* (1990)

Read on

A Man in Full; *Radical Chic* (NF)

Martin Amis, ***Money***; Michael Lewis, ***Liar's Poker*** (NF); ›› Norman Mailer, *The Deer Park*

TOBIAS WOLFF (b. 1945) USA

OLD SCHOOL (2003)

Perhaps the only institution more English than an English private school is an American one. Tobias Wolff's autobiographical novel is set in one such alma mater where virtually every student aspires to be the next ›› Hemingway, for the ultimate honour is to gain, through literary achievement, an audience with a visiting author. When Hemingway himself is announced as the final guest of the year, the narrator purloins and adapts a story written five years earlier by a pupil at the local girls' school. His entry is a clear winner but the truth soon emerges and he is summoned to the headmaster's office to confront his fate.

Goss, president of the Student Honour Council, accuses the narrator of dishonouring their class (although he appears more distraught at the fact that it is a girl's story that has been defrauded). Honour is the key here: the idea that rules are framed by and depend upon this concept goes unquestioned by the boys and it takes a teacher, Mr Ramsey, to expose it as pretentious nonsense. Agreeing that rule-breaking deserves punishment, Ramsey nevertheless demands that honour is left out of the matter. This is the narrator's first true lesson in the development of a privileged young man in sixties America. His second comes from the original author of the prize-winning story, who discourses on the predatory, arrogant and self-centred behaviour of boys at inter-school dances.

The final part of the book is observed from the point of view of the school's Dean, reluctantly instrumental in punishing the miscreant hero. It illustrates how we do not always learn from the lessons of our youth and that vanity, unconscious or otherwise, can make fools of us all.

Predominantly, Wolff is a writer of short stories and this discipline lends his longer books an economical style that greatly benefits the pace of the plot. He fought in Vietnam with the US Special Forces, this experience colouring his work not only with a sense of brotherhood but also one of betrayal and failure.

Read on

This Boy's Life (1993); *The Night in Question*

Nancy Kleinbaum, *Dead Poets Society*

SIR CLIVE WOODWARD (b. 1956) UK

WINNING (2004) (NF)

It's not often that a United Kingdom country wins anything in sport, let alone a World Cup, so whatever you think of the man, Clive Woodward must have something worthwhile to say. A sparkling if erratic international centre three-quarter in his day, Woodward revolutionised the way rugby union is organised in England after taking over the team in 1998. As non-English Lions players remarked in 2005, he was a manager rather than a coach. Instead, he hired coaches – coach-loads of them. Woodward's skill lay in the ability to win or, more precisely, to achieve conditions necessary to beat the best teams in the world home and away on a regular basis. The astonishing series of victories up to and through the 2003 World Cup are testimony to this painstaking work.

More than anything, Woodward's book highlights the many obstacles that, in his view, were placed in his way by a ruling body loath to cast off the trappings of amateurism. On his first day, he was stunned to find that he was not even to be provided with an office. His stubborn insistence on change riled many and some found him arrogant, but his attention to detail was critical in England's success. For instance, had he not included a lawyer in his World Cup entourage, his team might have been thrown out of the tournament for inadvertently fielding a sixteenth player for a brief period.

Men are naturally competitive. We love to win and there are few things more satisfying than doing so in a sporting context. ***Winning*** is not simply a well-written book about a manly sport; it is also a business text with valuable tips for running a successful organisation. It just happens to be about a rugby team and is perhaps all the more accessible for that reason.

Read on

Will Carling and Robert Heller, ***The Way to Win: Strategies in Business and Sport*** (NF); Martin Johnson, ***Martin Johnson*** (NF); Stephen Jones, ***On My Knees*** (NF); Donald McRae, ***Winter Colours*** (NF)

INDEX